# *Discovering*
## NORTHERN
# LAKELAND

# *Discovering*
# NORTHERN
# LAKELAND

## CHARLIE EMETT & JAMES TEMPLETON

The
History
Press

*Dedicated to three Cumberland Lasses,*
*Frances, Elizabeth and Anne.*

*Title page:* 'Solitude', Crummock Water.

First published 2009

The History Press
The Mill, Brimscombe Port
Stroud, Gloucestershire, GL5 2QG
www.thehistorypress.co.uk

British Library Cataloguing in Publication Data.
A catalogue record for this book is available from the British Library.

ISBN 978 0 7509 5083 1

Typesetting and origination by The History Press
Printed in Great Britain

# Contents

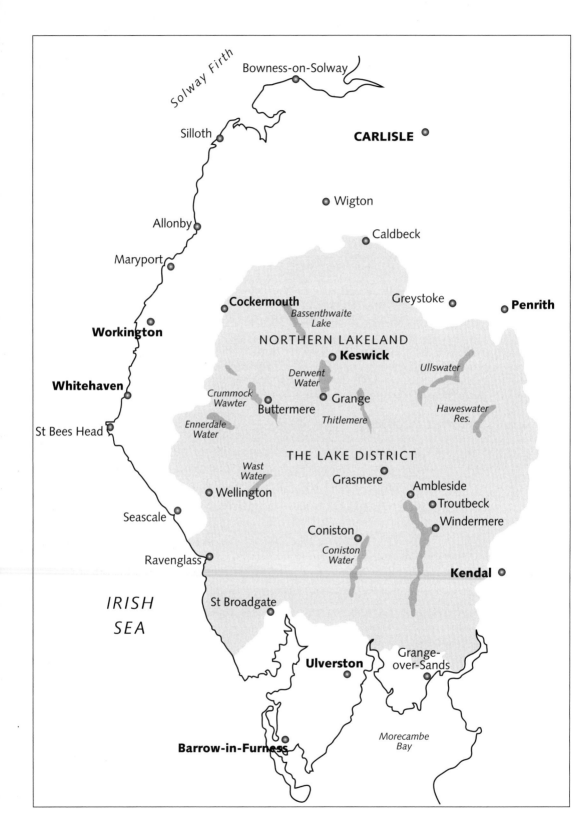

Solway Firth

Bowness-on-Solway

CARLISLE

Silloth

Wigton

Caldbeck

Allonby

Greystoke

Penrith

Cockermouth
*Bassenthwaite Lake*

Maryport

NORTHERN LAKELAND

Workington

Keswick

*Derwent Water*

*Ullswater*

Whitehaven

*Crummock Wawter*

Buttermere

Grange

*Haweswater Res.*

*Thitlemere*

St Bees Head

*Ennerdale Water*

THE LAKE DISTRICT

*Wast Water*

Grasmere

Wellington

Ambleside

Troutbeck

Seascale

Windermere

Coniston

Ravenglass

*Coniston Water*

Kendal

IRISH
SEA

St Broadgate

Ulverston

Grange-over-Sands

*Morecambe Bay*

Barrow-in-Furness

# Introduction

Cumberland, in the north-west corner of England, was controlled until after AD 1000 by both Scotland and England. Northern Cumberland came under the power of Scotland and looked to the Scottish See of Glasgow as its ecclesiastical authority; many North Cumberland churches were dedicated to Celtic saints associated with that diocese.

Among the first people to settle in this impoverished land were an uneasy mix of British, Anglican and, in about AD 900, Norse-Irish (the Vikings), who arrived via Ireland and the west. More than any other settlers, it was the Norse-Irish who made their mark on Cumberland, where their occupation is still reflected in groups of Cumbrian place names.

The Vikings were tough and succeeded in wrestling a scanty living from land which had not been cultivated before or had been barren for many years. This was the poorest part of England and those who worked the land lived in abject poverty despite their hard work. Down the centuries this north-west corner of England remained a lonely, barely identifiable region, sparsely populated by hardies who scraped a meagre living in a hostile environment.

Until about 1650 the Cumberland Mountains were regarded as places to be avoided because they were so unpleasant. What was needed was a change of attitude to the landscape which was to be brought about by the Romantic Poets led by William Wordsworth and Samuel Taylor Coleridge. Through their poems and other literary celebrations of the wonders of Cumberland's rural solitude, increasing numbers of 'comers' ventured into this wilderness to discover for themselves the mesmerising beauty of what today is renowned as the English Lake District. Before the end of the seventeenth century, the Romantic idyll had faded away. But in the hamlets work went on much as it always had done.

Then, along came steam. The effects of the railways on Cumberland were profound in that they played a major part in opening up the area. However, their blessings were mixed. Aspatria, 20 miles south-west of Carlisle, complained that cheap excursion trains were draining away local trade. Carlisle benefited from railway development by becoming a railway centre in which diverse enterprises used cheap railway transport. Extensions through the Cumbrian Mountains to places such as Silloth, Keswick and Workington opened the area up to mass tourism. Keswick in particular was quick to develop tourism for the better-heeled. It became a centre from where 'wealthier', educated people could experience small-scale explorations and the nearby lakes. From these beginnings, interest in the Cumberland Mountains grew. For the more daring visitors, the enigmatic way the heights folded one behind the other added mysticism and enchantment; people wanted to see what the hidden places had to offer. In this respect, one man more than any other opened up this mostly hidden countryside for almost everyone to enjoy. That man was Alfred Wainwright, fell walker extraordinaire, whose name is synonymous with the Lake District.

The whole of the Lake District, in the northern half of which this book is set, covers a picturesque mountainous region 30 miles by 25 miles in extent. In it are several tall peaks, including Scafell Pike which, at 3,210ft is the highest in England. Then there are the sixteen lakes after which the Lake District is named, plus its many tarns. From this exquisite blend emerges a natural beauty unsurpassed anywhere else in England. The whole of the Lake District, most of which is owned by the National Trust, was designated a national park in 1951.

A fine day for clipping sheep in 1898.

# 1

# The Cumbrian Plain

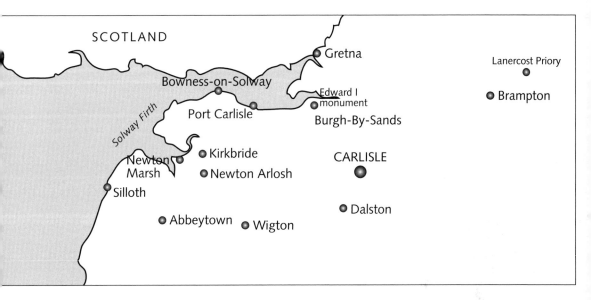

## LANDSCAPE AND CLIMATE

Northern Lakeland is the top half of England's most celebrated and most visited scenic area. It is just 30 miles across, yet twelve million visitors a year pour in to visit its famous lakes, picturesque villages and mountainous landscape. England's highest mountain, Scafell Pike and its largest and deepest lakes, Windermere and Wastwater respectively, are to be found there. The contrast between its spectacular, steep-sided peaks, its forested valleys, its lakes and glacial tarns, its wild fells and its dry-stone walled farmland is breathtaking in its diversity. Most of the land in Northern Lakeland is open fell and it is this landscape that attracts most visitors.

Here, as elsewhere, the vegetation is determined by the underlying soil but on the open fell this is less developed by man than the valleys.

Rough grassland is widespread on the open fell and this is sometimes carpeted with ling heather that paint the hillsides a glorious purple.

Northern Lakeland's weather is more diverse than that of any other area in England. The Lakeland Mountains are reputed to be the wettest place in Britain with an average annual rainfall of 170in. However, away from the high summits, the rainfall is much the same as any other part of England. Because Northern Lakeland is mainly mountainous and sited leeward of a wide expanse of ocean that is uncharacteristically warm for its latitude, it has fairly warm winter temperatures and rather cool summers. The north-east facing short valleys tend to hold snow well into June or July.

No matter what the weather is like or what views Cumbria has on offer, there is no better way to start a Northern Lakeland day than with a hearty breakfast of ham and eggs.

The morning hunt. A moderate wind disperses the fox's scent making the chase difficult for the hounds.

Mrs Ida Brough of Nook Farm, Southerney, with a hearty breakfast plate full of ham and eggs, pictured in about 1955. Her farmhouse kitchen, complete with her cat warming itself, is a typically North Lakeland scene.

# SILLOTH

## AT THE MOUTH OF THE SOLWAY FIRTH

The building of the Carlisle to Silloth railway in 1856, and the construction of a dock at Silloth in 1859, transformed a windswept coastal village into a busy port with a strong Canadian connection.

A summer day on Silloth Green, 1910.

Silloth pier. The ball is up, the tide is full and the sailing ship is well down in the water, loaded with grain.

Carrs of Carlisle, renowned biscuit-makers, got their grain from Canada, which also became an outlet for their biscuits. Both the grain and the biscuits were carried across the Atlantic in sailing ships whose English destination was Silloth. While the sailing ships were operating, Silloth did good business. However, this was short-lived. Now, Silloth has reverted to being a quiet seaside resort.

Sister Lily, who took between twenty and thirty under-privileged children to Silloth by train every weekend to sample a better life.

Mr Selkirk's shop.

Pierrots in Happy Valley, Silloth.

During the first half of the twentieth century, a remarkable lady, Sister Lily, brought disadvantaged children from all over Cumberland to spend a weekend holidaying with her in Silloth. She had a hut on the seafront where the children were accommodated. For her dedication to under-privileged children over many years, Sister Lily was awarded the OBE.

Every summer season Mr Selkirk ordered six tons of rock for his shop in Silloth. He sold it in 6in and 2in sizes. He also had a large show-stick on display in his window, which he broke up at the end of the season. He gave the pieces to Sister Lily for the poor children.

Being a seaside resort, Silloth had its Silloth Pierrots – David Fuller and his Merry Men and Maids. Here are their greetings from The Happy Valley, Silloth in this verse by E.A. Ferguson:

> Oh! There's such a Happy Valley by the Solway,
> When the golden, summer hours are on the wing,
> Where beside the waves the happy people gather,
> While the merry men and maids so sweetly sing,
> And listening hearts – respondent as the echo –
> Fall 'neath the spell that's over everything.

## BOWNESS-ON-SOLWAY                    *OS Grid Ref: NY225628*

### ON THE SOUTH BANK OF THE SOLWAY FIRTH

Hadrian's Wall passed through where Bowness-on-Solway now stands, but today there is no sign of it although some of the stones from the wall were used in the building of the parish church, St Mary's, which dates from the twelfth century. St Mary's stands on the highest part of Bowness and from it, across the estuary, interesting parts of Galloway can be seen, for example where, during the First World War, 'devil's porridge' was produced at the largest munitions factory in the world. It opened in 1915 and employed more than 30,000 people. 'Devil's porridge' was a highly explosive mixture of nitro-glycerine and nitro-cotton. It was dried, changed into cordite and put into shells and bullets.

Gretna Green can be seen to the north-east. Weddings are still conducted there in the old blacksmith's shop.

Having spent 700 years in St Mary's Church, the bells of St Mary's were stolen by the Scots, an incident commemorated in a poem called 'The Tenor Bell Makes A Request'.

A railway, built to convey iron ore from mines in the Whitehaven area to the steel works at Annan in Scotland, was carried from Bowness across the Solway Firth over a 1 mile 700yd-long viaduct. In 1881, during a severe winter, pressure of ice that had formed around the viaduct became so severe that it caused a long section of the viaduct to collapse, leaving the railway line hanging like a thread over the water; more money was spent on repairing this viaduct than on any other.

Bowness-on-Solway has a variation on the theme that many inns and churches have been built close together. Slightly east of the King's Arms, an altar is set into a wall.

Bowness-on-Solway. The bus, *c.* 1900.

Solway Viaduct, 1¼ miles long. Note the bee hives against the wall in the foreground.

A train crossing Solway Viaduct.

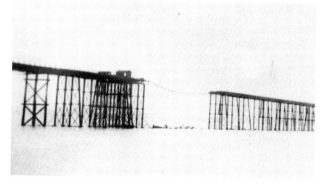

Damage caused to the Solway Viaduct by ice, 1881. The railway line is long like a thread.

Edward I monument with Scottish border hills in the background.

*Left:* King Edward I, 1239–1307, the 'Hammer of the Scots'. *Right:* A close-up of Edward I monument on Burgh Marsh.

# EDWARD I MONUMENT

*OS Grid Ref: NY326609*

## ALMOST ¾ OF A MILE NORTH OF BURGH BY SANDS

Edward I, known as Longshanks, the son of Henry III, was born in 1239 and became one of the most capable kings of medieval England. His ambition was to become king of the whole of Britain. This was only partly fulfilled with Wales being conquered and held in subjection with the aid of such castles as those in Caernarvon and Conway. In Scotland, Edinburgh supported the candidature of John Balliol for the throne, but his protégé was deposed in 1295. Edward invaded Scotland but although he became known as the 'Hammer of the Scots' and set up an English government in Scotland, he was opposed first by William Wallace and, after Wallace's execution, by Robert Bruce who troubled Edward's last years.

Edward journeyed north to re-establish his authority once he realised that a major campaign against the Scots was needed. He travelled during the summer of 1306, but he was not in a fit state of health for such a campaign. However, he was so determined to defeat the Scots that on 3 July, he set out from Carlisle. By now Edward was suffering from dysentery and his progress was hardly 2 miles a day. He spent the night of 6 July 1307 on Burgh Marsh. When, on 7 July 1307, his servants came to lift him out of bed so that he could eat, he died in their arms.

A wooden monument was built on the spot, but it rotted – as did another replacement wooden one. Then, in the eighteenth century, a stone monument was erected to replace them, financed partly by Lord Lonsdale. The stone monument began to tilt and a local girl wrote to the queen, who arranged for it to be straightened.

## THE SOLWAY FIRTH                    *OS Grid Ref: between NY050630 and NY350630*

### 5 MILES NORTH-EAST OF CARLISLE

The Eden, one of the most beautiful rivers in England, flows gracefully into the Solway Firth through a countryside of breathtaking beauty. It edges Burgh Marsh to merge with the River Esk and the pair of them are swallowed by the Irish Sea. The salt flats through which these rivers flow to form the Solway Firth and are an exceptionally important reserve for wading birds. Shelduck, Greylag and, more commonly, Pink-Footed geese nest there on migration. As sure as the harvest moon arrives each year, the first of the wild geese arrive to winter on this 'muddy ford', which is what the name 'Solway Firth' means.

The wild geese arrive in large numbers and settle on the Solway salt marshes, living almost exclusively on various grasses. While one of a pair is feeding or resting, the other is on guard. When danger threatens, the one on guard gives a warning cry. Wild geese are gregarious and have a complex social life which is expressed by the different calls they make, just like a domestic goose. They spend a lot of time on the salt flats of the Solway Firth, just going to the water to drink, for bathing and when danger threatens.

Salmon returning to spawn in the Rivers Eden and Esk usually face half-net fishers waiting to catch them in the Solway Firth on the running tide. The fishermen lower their half-nets across the salmon runs and many fish are caught in them. Half-net fishing is unique to the Solway Firth.

Greylag geese in flight near Bowness-on-Solway.

In medieval times, the route across the Solway Firth between England and Scotland was used on a regular basis.

During the Second World War, tall poles were erected all over the salt marshes to discourage landings by enemy aircraft.

Wild George McPherson and James Templeton on a very cold day on the Solway Firth.

Half-net fishers after salmon on the Solway Firth near the Eden estuary.

# LANERCOST PRIORY

## NORTH-EAST OF CARLISLE

Lanercost Priory was founded by Robert de Vallibus in about 1169. A tablet at the west end of the church gives the date as 1116, but this is not correct.

Edward I, the 'Hammer of the Scots', stayed there in 1280 and in 1306, when the priory was in its prime. Ever intent on expanding, by force, his control of all Britain, Edward made frequent forays into Scotland, using Lanercost Priory as his base, much to the distress of the peace-loving monks.

In 1306, Edward, whose objective was to harry Robert Bruce, took ill at Lanercost Priory which was a costly time for the monks. Edward had with him 7 valets, 23 packhorse drivers who were responsible for the royal household's goods, 45 drivers and 22 grooms for the general luggage, 59 servants responsible for work in the kitchen, buttery, armoury and other departments as well. In all, 200 people had to be accommodated. Edward's condition worsened and his stay at Lanercost Priory became so extended that the monks feared that they would never see the end of them all.

*Above:* Replicas of King Edward I and his second wife, Queen Eleanor, in the north-west corner of Lanercost Priory. They were there shortly before his death on Burgh Marsh on 7 July 1307.

*Above, right:* Lakeland farmworkers and shepherds. The boss is wearing a bowler hat.

*Right:* Country ladies enjoying themselves on a home-made see-saw, a plank balanced on a saw-horse, 1906.

Having worked up an appetite, the ladies enjoy tea.

However, Edward was determined to get to grips with Robert Bruce and, despite his ill health eventually moved on to Carlisle.

Robert Bruce invaded England in 1311, attacked Lanercost Priory and left it ruinous. Then, in 1346, David, King of the Scots, also invaded England and he left the priory ruined and crippled for ever after.

Following the Dissolution of the Monasteries in 1536, Lanercost Priory was given to the Dacres of Lanercost who made their manor house out of part of the buildings. For 200 years most of the priory remained ruinous. Then, part of it was restored in the guise of the parish church which still stands. The church is a delight and the ruins are an interesting reminder of the 'Hammer of the Scots'.

## THE DEBATABLE LANDS

For more than 350 years, the area around Carlisle, incorporating the Cumbrian Plain, was known as the Debatable Land: the area was repeatedly plundered by invading Scots. Resulting from almost ceaseless raids and counter raids, Cumbrian farmers fared badly. To a large degree, their farms were separated from distant markets except for livestock, which could be driven over long distances to reach them. There was little urban and industrial development here, as in other parts of England, and there were very few places where farmers could sell their products.

By the late eighteenth century, many small farmers in Cumbria were castigated for lack of improvement and for 'seeming to inherit with the estates, their ancestors' notions of cultivating them.' Static local demand created no incentive to increase crops or adopt new methods which might include recommended rotations of crops like clover or turnips. Moreover, much of the land was wet and many small farmers could not afford expensive drainage.

It was not until the end of the eighteenth century that high wartime food prices enabled Cumberland farmers to move on to a more commercial footing. By 1810, an increasing number of Cumbrian folk were living in towns. This stimulated farming, especially in the Cumbrian Plain, and was the start of a farming transformation which was achieved within a generation. Many village fields and large areas of common land were enclosed. The overall effort was that during the Napoleonic Wars, Cumbria changed from a grain importer to an exporter.

This 'great re-building' of Cumbrian farms brought rising living standards. Many farmers invested in new buildings for over-wintering cattle. Along the main drove roads cattle markets developed and Cumberland farming was looking up.

## PORT CARLISLE                    *OS Grid Ref: NY242622*

### 1 MILE SOUTH-EAST OF BOWNESS-ON-SOLWAY

Between 1819 and 1823 a canal was built from Carlisle to a harbour at Fisher's Cross, some 5 miles away (to the west-south-west), on the south bank of the Solway Firth. Fisher's Cross was a hamlet of two houses and a pub called the Binnacle Inn. The canal was designed to provide a better link between the Solway Firth and Carlisle than the River Eden offered because it was not deep enough to accommodate large sea-going vessels. When the canal was completed, Fisher's Cross was renamed Port Carlisle. Locks 18ft wide were built into the canal, which made it wide enough to take large vessels.

'Port Carlisle possesses a railway, perforce, where the sole locomotive is a commonplace horse.
And in all merry England there's surely no other train system with so little danger or bother.
So here's to the creature that's useful and handy, Success and renown still attend the old Dandy.'

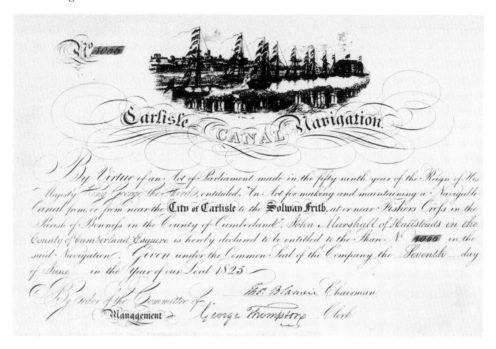

A copy of a share certificate for the Carlisle Canal.

Transferring cargo from the larger vessel to the smaller one for its onward journey along the Carlisle Canal to Carlisle.

However, it was not deep enough for them, so it was common practice for cargo to be transferred at Port Carlisle into smaller vessels for the final part of their journey to Carlisle. For a while the canal prospered, but by the 1840s the canal was hard hit by railway competition. After 1848 no dividend was paid and in 1853 the canal was drained and a railway was built on its bed.

A loop line was built from Port Carlisle to Drumburgh, some 4 miles west of Burgh by Sands, along which a danby (a railway carriage pulled by a horse) ran a regular service. One passenger, a lady who used to sit at the side of the carriage with her feet dangling in the trackside grass, said it was delightful and made her feel good.

By 1854 the railway had become redundant as well. Now all that is left is a footpath that has become part of the Hadrian's Wall path.

## CARLISLE'S PORT ROAD BASIN                   *OS Grid Ref: NY398564*

SOUTH OF THE RIVER EDEN AT THE NORTHERN END OF CARLISLE
At the eastern end of the 11¼-mile-long Carlisle Canal, the men whose ships carried grain, stone, coal and timber into Carlisle, relaxed in the Jovial Sailor; the air was filled with the sound of their banter and laughter.

It all began in 1794 when several businessmen with a dream met at the Queen's Head, Newcastle, to make plans for a canal that would run from Newcastle to Carlisle, then on to Stansfield. The canal would carry vessels with a cargo of up to 60 tons and link the east and west coasts of Britain.

The *Robert Burns* leaving Carlisle along the Carlisle Ship Canal, bound for Port Carlisle.

Ships in the Port Road Basin, Carlisle. The castle and the cathedral are in the background. The vessels carried loads of up to 60 tons.

However, the ambitious plan fell through, although a more feasible canal was proposed to run from Fisher's Cross to Carlisle. It would cost £71,000 to build and would produce revenue of £7,000 per annum.

From the start, there was some opposition, and when one of the canal cottages was set on fire, the canal company offered a reward of £20.

When the canal opened on 12 March 1823, the city was deserted; all the shops were closed and a crowd of 25,000 gathered at the basin for the official opening ceremony.

The canal was 54ft wide and contained eight locks. When it crossed a road, there were draw bridges with a bridge-master's house alongside. It was the bridge-master's job to raise his bridge to allow the tall-masted ships to pass through.

By the 1840s business had declined to almost nothing and in 1853 the canal was drained. The importance of Carlisle's Port Road basin shrank as a result of railway competition, although there were some who put the blame for ruining the chances of the Carlisle Canal on the building of docks at Silloth.

## CARLISLE CASTLE                      *OS Grid Ref: NY398564*

NEAR THE NORTHERN END OF CARLISLE, SOUTH OF THE RIVER EDEN
In the twelfth century, Henry I decided to build a castle at Carlisle to defend the most northerly outpost of England. He chose for it a hill overlooking the Eden. Three Roman forts had already been built on the hill at three different times. During the Edwardian

times the castle grew and its Tile Tower, as well as other extensions, was added by Richard III while he was still Duke of Gloucester. The Tile Tower was built into the wall which runs from the castle to join the west walls of the city. The interior of the castle was adapted to accommodate cannon during the reign of Henry VIII.

In 1568, Mary Queen of Scots was imprisoned there. It was not a strict captivity for she was a feisty lady who did not take kindly to the restrictions of captivity that her cousin Queen Elizabeth had imposed upon her. Sir Francis Knollys was her gaoler, a task he did not relish. He decided that if he gave her certain freedoms it would make life easier for himself. So he allowed her to go riding and to watch her courtiers play football on the castle green. When Mary was sent to more secure imprisonment at Bolton Castle, it was Sir Francis Knollys who gave the greatest sigh of relief.

In 1745, Bonnie Prince Charlie, with his army, entered Carlisle en route to invade England. He would go as far south as Derby before being driven back. At the Battle of Culloden in Inverness-shire his army was defeated and he fled, first to Skye, then to France.

General view of Carlisle Castle.

The Border Regiment band beating the retreat for the last time in front of Carlisle Castle. It is now amalgamated with the Duke of Lancashire Regiment, becoming The Duke of Lancashire Regiment, (Kings), Lancaster and Border Regiment. Carlisle people still consider Carlisle Castle to be home to the Border Regiment and the regimental museum is housed there.

Three hundred and eighty-two prisoners were sent to Carlisle for trial where they were imprisoned in the castle in darkness and with little food or water. Twenty were hanged, had their entrails burnt, their heads chopped off and were exposed over the Scottish gate of the city. One, it is said, was a lad with long yellow hair. Every morning and evening an unknown lady came to look at the head. Then, one day, both the head and the lady vanished, never to be seen again.

On one occasion when a highland regiment had to pass through Carlisle, it was halted outside the city so that the men might not see the heads.

## CARLISLE CATHEDRAL                                            *OS Grid Ref: NY398560*

NORTH-WEST CARLISLE, SOUTH OF THE RIVER EDEN

Of all the English cathedrals, only Oxford Cathedral is smaller than Carlisle, which was built on a site provided by Henry I as a priory for Augustinians in 1133. Henry I made Carlisle the see of a bishop and the priory then became Carlisle Cathedral, the only Augustinian house in England to have achieved such status. The south transept and the nave, now the Border Regiment Chapel, are about all that remains of the original building. The Normans added to the cathedral, using stones taken from Hadrian's Wall and the remains of Luguvallum; this contrasts strongly with the red sandstone that was added during later building. In 1292, a serious fire damaged the cathedral and the rebuilding that followed included the magnificent fourteenth-century east window, considered to be one of the finest in Europe. By the end of the fourteenth century, more detailed work had been added by Bishop William Strickland, who was responsible for the north transept and the cathedral's squat tower, which then had a spire.

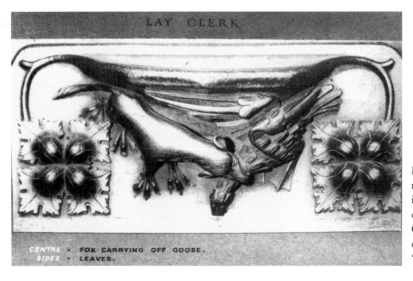

Medieval misericords in the choir of Carlisle Cathedral. This one is called 'Lay Clerk'.

Medieval misericord in the choir of Carlisle Cathedral. This one is called 'The Town Clerk'.

It was in Carlisle Cathedral that Edward I solemnly used bell, book and candle to excommunicate Robert Bruce and when Bonnie Prince Charlie entered Carlisle in 1745, the cathedral bells were rung in welcome. Carlisle was playing safe. During the Civil War, Carlisle was the chief Royalist stronghold in the north. Parliamentarians laid siege to it for eight months, the longest siege in the city's history. As the siege developed, Parliamentarian troops demolished six of the cathedral's bays and used the stone to repair the city walls and the castle. The truncated nave was later walled off. It was still in poor repair in 1797 when Sir Walter Scott was married there.

The Victorians carried out much restoration work with great sensitivity. The cathedral's beautifully painted deep blue ceiling with its gold stars is the work of Owen Jones, who also replaced many of the coats of arms of local families that were originally on the medieval roof. Medieval misericords carved into the canopied choir stalls represent weird animals and birds: two dragons joined by their ears, pelicans feeding their young, a fox killing a goose and a mermaid with a looking-glass. How's that for originality!

## THE EAST WINDOW, CARLISLE CATHEDRAL

Carlisle Cathedral is a fragment of the Priory Church, which was founded in about 1123. In 1225 the cathedral was largely extended, but in 1292 a serious fire, fanned by a gale, seriously damaged the cathedral, as it did the whole of Carlisle. The choir, which the fire destroyed, was gradually rebuilt on a grand scale, giving the cathedral many of its decorated Gothic features, the finest example of which was the fantastic tracery of the east window. Little of the original glass survived and it is little short of miraculous that the tracery did.

In 1882, Mr Freeman at the Carlisle Congress of the Royal Archaeological Institute said of the east window that it was the grandest of its kind in England and, he supposed, in the world.

There was as big a window in one of the churches in Perugia, which in some ways reminded him of this, but here they had the finest piece of tracery to be seen anywhere. Next to it came the Abbey Church of Selby which, however, was smaller. He continued, 'in this choir might be seen one distinctive English peculiarity, the absence of a vault in so great a church.' The English tradition of making a wooden roof ornamental feature was here to be seen on the greatest scale.

*Left:* The east window, Carlisle Cathedral. *Right:* A rare picture of Carlisle Cathedral's east window, highlighting its wonderful tracery and stained glass.

## TULLIE HOUSE, CARLISLE                    *OS Grid Ref: NY396564*

MIDWAY BETWEEN THE CASTLE AND THE CATHEDRAL
Tullie house is Carlisle's award-winning museum and art gallery. For anyone wishing to explore the background to this historic city, Tullie House is not to be missed. It was built in 1699 by the Tullies, a German family, part of three or four hundred miners who made

Tullie House, with Carlisle Cathedral behind, seen from Carlisle Castle.

In about 1910, when this picture was taken, Carlisle ladies backed their men-folk by providing a secure base for them. Occasionally, they treated themselves to an outing. These ladies from St Mary's Church are ready for such an outing.

their fortunes in mines around Keswick The local landed gentry did not take kindly to these foreigners, but prospects were good for the Germans so they remained in their new country. When Tullie House was built in 1699, it was the finest mansion of that time in Carlisle. It stands in the middle of Carlisle's historic quarter, a compact area that is intersected with ancient thoroughfares.

At Tullie House, Carlisle's 2,000-year history can be traced. In Tullie House you discover that the Romans used Carlisle as a base. Of all the settlements along the wall, only Carlisle became a city. Detailed information about the Roman occupation of Carlisle is available at Tullie House, as is the spellbinding story of, what may now be peaceful and beautiful countryside, but which used to be the 'Debatable Lands', home to the warring Reivers.

Tullie House also houses an extensive collection of Roman remains from Carlisle itself and from the Cumbrian part of Hadrian's Wall.

Eden Bridge, Carlisle, upstream of which the River Eden ceases to be tidal. Between Eden Bridge and Rickerby Park the river is noted for the salmon found there.

A springer, (a young salmon), caught by James Templeton, spinning a cock-leggy fly, at Rickerby Rocks on the Eden in 1968. It weighed 18lb.

The art gallery houses a host of very interesting exhibits, including paintings by Pre-Raphaelite artists. Tullie House is not just a pretty place; it is a treasure house.

## CARLISLE CITY CENTRE                    *OS Grid Ref: NY402557*

SOUTH OF EDEN BRIDGE

As Caerluel, Carlisle was a British capital for 250 years after the Normans left. It was associated with Cunedda, the first great king of the Western Cumbri and Rhydderch the Magnificent who extended his power from there over all Strathclyde in the sixth century. In addition to all that, legend has it that 'King Arthur lived at merry Carlisle.' It is assumed that local kings traditionally remembered in the Arthurian romances made

The Guildhall, Carlisle, pictured in 2000.

Carlisle City Centre and Carlisle Cross, erected in 1632.

Carlisle their headquarters. By AD 680 the Angles were dominant in Carlisle and it was they who gave it to St Cuthbert.

Nothing much is left of Anglican Carlisle. It was rendered ruinous in AD 876 and it was not until 1092 that William Rufus drove out the Anglicans and colonised the town afresh.

Strong walls once enclosed Carlisle. The West Walls, built from 1122, are all that remain, but they are a fine example of what these defences looked like.

The Guildhall Museum, built in 1407, was once a meeting place of the medieval trade guilds. In it today, the commercial success of what is now the city of Carlisle is revealed.

The Old Town Hall, which dates from 1717, is where Carlisle's award-winning Tourist Information Centre is sited.

English Street, Carlisle, in about 1910, cobbled and with tram lines.

Looking into English Street from the Courts on the occasion of Queen Victoria's diamond jubilee, 1897. The triumphal arch was decorated for the occasion.

Close to this historic quarter of Carlisle is the Citadel with its 'twin drum' bastions, built by Henry VIII.

Carlisle's historic city centre continues to evolve and increasingly plays a very important role in the business, social and cultural life of this great city.

## CITADEL STATION                    *OS Grid Ref: NY402555*

### SLIGHTLY SOUTH OF THE CITADEL

Often, people visiting Carlisle for the first time mistake the Citadel for Carlisle Castle. But this intimidating fortress, with its huge circular towers, was not built until 1543. Henry VIII ordered its construction to strengthen the city's defences. Most of it was demolished in the early 1800s to improve access to the city centre; but what remains is very impressive.

A montage depicting the seven railways that worked in and out of Carlisle's Citadel station.

Court Square Crescent wraps itself around the Citadel and, immediately south of it, Citadel station is sited. In 1836, the first railway to Carlisle opened, but Citadel station was not opened until 1850. It was built to serve seven different railway companies, whose coats of arms are still displayed on the station façade.

The line from Carlisle to Silloth was inspired by the city's desire for a new outlet to the sea. Between 1857 and 1859, new docks were built at Silloth, but railway revenue was poor so Silloth was developed as a seaside health resort for Carlisle and the Scottish Border and Lowlands – though without much success.

One of the last main line railways to be built in Britain, the famous Settle-Carlisle Railway had its northern terminus at Citadel station. The line was completed in 1876, is still operational, is 72 miles long and takes in some of the most dramatic scenery in the north of England.

Citadel station's interior was so elegant that it became known as 'the top hat'. Today it is still an important station. Trains from Glasgow and London link there with others to places like Dumfries, Tyneside, West Cumbria and Yorkshire.

## CARLISLE IN FLOOD

The beautiful River Eden meanders westwards between Rickerby Park and Edenside Cricket Club to the north, and golf courses and Bitts Park to the south. Two smaller rivers, the Petteril and Caldew, join it from the south. Carlisle city centre is bounded by them.

This is the shallow end of Carlisle. The traffic lights at the other end of the city were submerged. Houses in Caldewgate, pictured, fared badly; people in Warwick Road were homeless for months and most of Carlisle had no electricity for a week.

'The customer asked for a splash of water in his whisky, but this is ridiculous. I'll sack that new barman.'

As a rule, these three rivers know their place and stay in it. However, there are exceptions to every rule and January 2005 proved to be one. When it rains in Cumbria it doesn't use half measures. Yet, even by Cumbrian standards, the stormy wet weather of that January was exceptional. Dark, grey, rain-bearing nimbus clouds spread across the Carlisle area and along the full length of the Eden Valley like a sodden blanket, sagging with the weight of the rain that formed them.

The clouds burst and for several hours rain poured down, filling feeders to overflowing, browning the three rivers and making them angry. The waters rose swiftly and the rivers burst their banks. Carlisle, surprised by the speed of the water flooding its streets, found itself awash.

In the Willow Holme area the flooding reached a height of 15ft, reaching the top deck seats of double-decker buses in the bus depot. The city centre was cut off and the mayor was unable to rescue his chain of office from the safe in the Civic Centre, which was isolated by flood water.

When the flood waters reached the Solway, they met an exceptionally high tide, which acted as a barrier, causing the Eden to spill more water into Carlisle city centre. So severe was the flooding that hundreds of homes had to be evacuated and people in the Warwick Road area were homeless for months. Carlisle had no electricity for weeks and Edenside Cricket Club found a new meaning for 'ducks'.

## CARLISLE CHARACTERS

Today, for the most part, people tend to be confined within limits imposed by the politically correct element and are the poorer for it. However, a century ago things were very different. People were proud of their individuality, rejoiced in doing their own thing and took no notice of those interfering people who could not abide folk with minds of their own. Carlisle had its fair share of 'characters' and was the richer because of them.

Jimmy Dyer was a street character whose main haunt was Great Grapes Lane, one of several small streets leading off Lowther Street. On a daily basis he would play his violin to entertain passers by. His musical talent left much to be desired but his somewhat screechy renderings were well received. Jimmy had a second string to his bow; he would compose little songs, with which he entertained the passing throng. Jimmy was much missed when he died in 1907.

Jimmy Dyer in Great Grapes Lane, Carlisle, *c.* 1900.

Different aspects of Carlisle, home to many wonderful characters.

Carlisle character nicknamed 'Hay-fa-lads' by
the public because he called all men 'hay-fa-
lads' and all women 'straw-for-lasses'.

Another Carlisle character was in the habit of stopping buses and asking if they were
going to the North Pole. Because he invariably referred to all men as 'hay-fa-lads' and all
women as 'straw-for-lasses', usually shouted as he marched to Brunton Park, the public
gave him the nick-name 'Hay-fa-lads'.

He suffered from bunions so, to ease the pain, he cut the tops off his boots, exposing
his toes to the air. He would regularly visit The Pheasant for a 'tatie' pot meal with a pint.
When the meal was served, he would go to the bar for his drink, having first spat on his
'tatie' pie. This regular ritual was to ensure that no one else in the bar would sample his
meal while he was having a drink. The ploy worked; no-one ever tampered with his meal.

These two characters and others like them, by their odd behaviour, brought a little
sunshine into people's lives.

# THE JEW OF CARLISLE

William Henry Mounsey was born at the family seat of the Mounseys, newly built Castletown House, a nineteenth-century villa superbly sited on the edge of the River Eden almost a mile west of Rockliffe church (OS Grid Ref: NY348620). The year was 1808. He died there sixty-nine years later in 1877, having lived an extraordinary life.

As a boy he took interest in mazes on Rockliffe Marsh and this highlighted his fondness for all things strange and obscure.

He became an accomplished linguist being able to converse fluently in Greek, Latin, Persian and Welsh, as well as his own tongue.

When he was sevnteen years old, William Mounsey joined the Army and much of his military service was spent in the Middle East where he came into regular contact with a great many Jews. He made a profound study of the Jewish way of life, history and religion.

On leaving the Army and the Navy, Captain Mounsey became a solicitor in the family firm, a position he held for the remainder of his eventful life. This suited him because it was lucrative enough to enable him to indulge in the eccentricities for which he would be remembered long after his death.

He began to dress like a Jew, wore his beard in the Jewish fashion and generally acted the part so well that, at a time when no Jew lived in or around Carlisle, he became known as 'The Jew of Carlisle'.

His strange behaviour was not confined to the way he dressed and grew his beard. He took to chiselling enigmatic inscriptions on the sandstone cliffs of Eden Gorge and other places.

Yet, although the name 'William Mounsey' is perpetuated in his strange rock carvings, it is for his famous pilgrimage from the Solway Marshes in search of the source of the Eden that he is best remembered. That and the Jew Stone, a puzzling monument that he had erected near the Eden's source in praise of the Jews.

Captain William Mounsey RN, one of the famous Mounseys of Castletown 'Mansion'. Before joining the Royal Navy he was an officer in the Army.

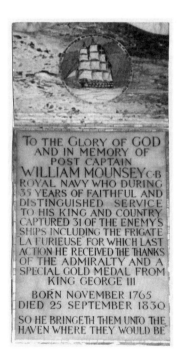

This plaque and portrait in Rockcliffe church are both dedicated to the remarkable William Mounsey. The special medal from King George III was of pure gold and was a one-off.

Castletown House, family seat of the Mounseys, known locally as Castletown Mansion.

## DALSTON VILLAGE                                    *OS Grid Ref: NY370501*

### 3½ MILES SOUTH OF CARLISLE

Dalston is a village built around a pele tower that was the seat of the Dalstons. The pele tower has now been enlarged into a mansion, to the north and west of which there is an ancient rampart and ditch, known as the Bishop's Dyke.

Prior to the Civil War throughout England, aristocratic and gentry dominance rested on the economic, social and political influence possessed by landowning families like the Musgraves of Edenhall, the Dacres, Curwens and the Dalstons. The influence of the Dalston, Musgrave and Lowther families extended to Westmorland. Even the emergency created by the Civil War, which broke out in August 1642, only briefly disturbed this state of affairs. There is no doubt about the tenacity with which these local oligarchies defended their dominance during this troubled period.

A very 'only country' event, maypole dancing, takes place in Dalston on a regular basis. The maypole has a permanent site in the middle of the village and whenever a village festival is held, the maypole invariably becomes the focal point for the festival's activities. There is something endearing about dancing around a maypole. The dancers enjoy weaving in and out of the ropes with intricate foot movements. Equally, those watching appear enthralled by the dancers' activities. Perhaps that's the secret. Apart from being fun to take part in, maypole dancing is, without doubt, a most enjoyable spectator event. Long may it continue to fascinate people, especially in Dalston, where it is much loved.

Maypole dancing at Dalston in the rain.

# THE CHURCH OF ST MICHAEL, BURGH BY SANDS

*OS Grid Ref:*
*NY321590*

## 5 MILES WEST OF CARLISLE

Built entirely of stone from a fort on Hadrian's Wall in 1181, the Church of St Michael is thought to be the earliest example of a fortified church. Its tower and walls are 7ft thick and were designed for protection against border raids. From the Church of St Michael, Galloway on the Scottish side of the Solway Firth can be seen.

St Michael's Church, Burgh by Sands, is one of only a few fortified churches. It is Norman except for the tower, which was rebuilt by Edward II.

In 1307, Edward I was already a dying man when he left Carlisle on 3 July, intent on defeating his old enemy, Robert Bruce. Progress was painfully slow and by 7 July he had travelled only a few miles. His intention was to cross the Solway Firth into Scotland at low tide but he never achieved it. On 7 July Edward died on the Solway Marches. Today, a monument marks the spot. His body was brought to Burgh by Sands and laid in the Church of St Michael.

The king's death and disputes between the barons in England allowed Robert Bruce to consolidate his position in Scotland.

When Edward II, who was much weaker than Edward I, moved north to attack the Scottish army, he was well and truly defeated at Bannockburn and his attempt to fulfil his father's ambition ended in failure.

Following Bannockburn, the Bishop of Carlisle made a private arrangement with the Scots for the protection of his own estates.

There is an iron door between St Michael's Church and the tower and over it there is an early lintel that is grotesquely carved on the underside.

Edward I window, St Michael's Church, Burgh by Sands. He reigned for thirty-six years and seven months and was sixty-eight when he died. He laid in state in St Michael's.

The Duke of Norfolk erected the first monument to Edward I at Burgh by Sands in 1685 but it collapsed in 1785. The present one was erected in July 2007.

## KIRKBRIDE

### 9 MILES WEST OF CARLISLE

Kirkbride is a very pretty village at the mouth of the River Wampool. Its name is derived from 'Kir-brydock' an Irish form of 'little dear Bridget' and its church is dedicated to St Bridget. Sir Walter Scott, Ruskin and Turner all loved the landscape in which Kirkbride is situated. Scott visited the place time and time again and used it as a background for his favourite creations.

Kirkbride has long been known for breeding game cocks and was once notorious as a place where cock fighting regularly took place. In a cock fight, specially bred and trained cocks were matched for stakes. They were equipped with spurs, usually of steel, and they fought until one of them was killed. The area which the fights took place was called a cockpit. Whenever there was a match between a number of birds on either side it was known as a 'main'. A 'main' in which the victory went to the side represented by the last survivor was known as a 'battle royal'. Cock fighting was made illegal in Britain in 1849 but it was still carried on secretly for many years afterwards. It probably still is.

Kirkbride is famous for curing bacon. Preserving the meat by salting and smoking is a skilled occupation and the people of Kirkbride have got it off to a fine tee.

The railway line from Carlisle to Silloth skirted Kirkbride, which had a small station. The line was very popular with people from the lowlands of south-west Scotland who used it when going to Silloth, a popular holiday resort. Today the line has been dismantled.

Kirkbride in about 1900. The boy, front right, is pushing the railway barrow.

## NEWTON ARLOSH
*OS Grid Ref: NY205555*

### ½ A MILE EAST OF NEWTON MARSH

The origin of Newton Arlosh is lost in the mists of time. Annals tell of an ancient church having been built there in about AD 400 by St Ninian; and that is about all that is known about it.

History is on much firmer ground when it records that the monks of Holm Cultram Abbey established the village of Newton Arlosh on the Solway Marshes in 1307 to replace the nearby market town of Skinburness, which had been used as a base for the navy of Edward I in 1299 in support of his attack on the Scots. The town was destroyed a few years later, taken by a terrible storm. What remained of Skinburness became a fishing village and Newton Arlosh was built to replace the town. The name Newton Arlosh means 'the new town on the marsh'.

James Templeton standing in the 2ft 7in wide doorway of St John's church, Newton Arlosh, the smallest church doorway in England.

The fortified church of St John, Newton Arlosh. Its pele tower and small doorway are clearly seen.

Work did not begin on building Newton Arlosh's church, St John's, until 1393. Because there was no castle close enough to protect the local population from border raids, the church was fortified and a pele tower was added to it. Other defences included making the church doorway only 2ft 7in wide and a little over 5ft high. This is believed to be the smallest church doorway in England. The church's 12in arrow-shot east window is also the smallest in England. So it was that St John's Church became one of the most delightful examples of a fortified church in the nation.

Following the Reformation, the church became derelict and was not restored until 1844.

Inside the church there is a fine eagle lectern, which is carved out of log oak.

## ABBEYTOWN AND THE BEE LADY            *OS Grid Ref: NY175509*

### 5 MILES WEST OF WIGTON

Abbeytown grew up around the famous twelfth-century Abbey of Holm Cultrum on the River Waver and most of the town's buildings are constructed of stone taken from the abbey when it became ruinous.

The abbey was founded about 1150 by Prince Henry, son of David I of Scotland, at a time when Cumberland was more Scottish than English; it was a great and wealthy place. The church was bigger than that of Carlisle. In it, seven priests could say Mass without interrupting one another. The present church is only about half the length of the original which, in 1216, was pillaged by the Scots who, returning to Scotland following this desecration, were all drowned by a sudden tide while crossing the Solway.

Telling the bees of a birth or a death in the family. This bee lady was photographed in the Abbeytown area in 1905.

Adjusting a hive of bees.

A bee keeper claiming a swarm of bees.

Abbeytown has long been associated with the bee lady. For centuries it had been traditional in many Cumberland towns and villages to inform the local bees about important events like births, marriages and deaths. If the bees were not informed of these happenings, ill fortune would threaten the place involved. So a lady was appointed to ensure that all these bees became aware of events in their particular area. It was a task that was regarded as very important for the welfare of the inhabitants and the bee lady was treated with great respect by her fellow beings.

The same respect was not shown by the bees themselves. They hated being disturbed and became very angry in thundery weather. This was a custom that went on throughout most of Cumberland and still happens in some villages. In Thursby village there are still some stone bee hives built into the garden wall of a lady who lives there.

## WIGTON

*OS Grid Ref: NY255485*

### 10 MILES SOUTH-WEST OF CARLISLE

Wigton has been a market town for centuries and is still a popular centre for social life between the Solway coast and the Cumbrian plain. Its prosperity is based on the weaving of cotton and linen. It was granted a Royal Charter in 1262 and a market is still held on Tuesdays. Annual horse sales are held in Wigton, riding horses and ponies being sold in April and heavy horses and ponies being sold in October.

Wigton parish church is said to have been built by Odard de Wigton, first baron, in the twelfth century, using materials from the Roman camp at Old Carlisle, now a farm,

The fountain at the centre of Wigton, dedicated to George Moore.

East End, Wigton

1½ miles south of Wigton. The Roman camp was huge and lay in a loop of the Wiza Beck. Many altars, inscriptions and the like have been found there. Wigton church was rebuilt in 1788 and contains monuments of the seventeenth and eighteenth centuries. Wigton Grammar School was built in 1730.

Local parishioners included Ewan Clark, the Cumbrian poet (1734–1811), and R. Smirke, the artist (1752–1845), father of Sir R. Smirke RA, the architect of Lowther Castle, the Eden bridges and Carlisle Court Houses to name but a few.

Most of this old town is a conservation area, in particular along Main Street. The upper stories of the buildings have survived in an almost unaltered state. On street corners, metal guards to prevent heavy horse-drawn wagons damaging the walls can still be seen.

## GEORGE MOORE, WIGTON BENEFACTOR

George Moore was born at Mealsgate, on 9 April 1806. At the age of thirteen, he became apprenticed to a Wigton draper called Messenger. George secretly gambled in a pub and when Messenger found out he tried to get rid of him. A caring lady, Nanny Graves, interceded for him and gave him lodgings. This incident changed George Moore's life. When he was eighteen, he went to London to seek his fortune. For a fortnight he walked the streets before being given employment with Fisher, Stroud and Robinson. Five years later, he was made a partner in the firm, now called Gravcock, Copestake, Moore and Company. On 12 August 1840, he married Liza Flint Ray.

In August 1844, on doctor's advice, he had a holiday in New York, where he met wealthy Joseph Blane, who had served his apprenticeship in Wigton at the same time as George Moore. They worked together on various successful business projects and George himself became very wealthy.

His wife wanted him to do something for Wigton so, after her death in December 1859, George helped to finance a factory there. Then he had a drinking fountain erected in the town.

George's second wife was Agnes, second daughter of Richard Breeks of Warcop, Westmorland. She was a loyal and noble wife.

On the last Sunday of his life, at the end of a walk in the garden with Potter, his faithful servant, George said to him, 'be sure and look after the poor people when I am gone.' Next day he cancelled a meeting in Aspatria to go to another in Carlisle regarding establishing a nurses' home. Mrs Moore was on this committee and said there was no need for him to attend. He replied, 'I must go, it will be the last time I shall be in Carlisle.'

They reached Carlisle about midday and Mrs Moore and a friend went shopping while George went to meet his friend, Mr Steel, of the *Carlisle Journal*. They were crossing the street opposite the Grey Goat Inn when two runaway horses galloped towards them at a furious rate. Steel reached the pavement but the second horse caught George, knocking him down. He fell heavily on his head and right side.

When George had left for London in 1825, he caught the coach from the Grey Goat and it was into this same coach that he was carried after having been knocked down by the horse. He died the next day. In his pocket was £50, intended as a subscription for the nurses' home.

Mealsgate village, birthplace of George Edward Moore.

Before the meeting in Carlisle, George had called at a music shop about a song he wanted for his wife. He could not remember the title so he hummed the tune. It was recognised by the shop assistant as 'The Harp Is Now Silent'.

## CALDBECK AND JOHN PEEL                    *OS Grid Ref: NY322399*

### 6 MILES SOUTH-EAST OF WIGTON

Caldbeck's greatest claim to fame is its association with John Peel, the renowned huntsman, who was born in a nearby cottage called Park End.

'D'ye Ken John Peel', the famous Cumberland hunting song, is known and sung in every quarter of the globe, but few people know its history. Despite the common notion arising from the erroneous alteration of the original and later editions, it was not 'at Troutbeck once on a day' but at Caldbeck in Cumberland that John Peel was born and buried. His coat was grey, not 'gay' as it is in the song, being home spun from the local Herdwick sheep.

John Peel, huntsman.

John Woodcock Graves, author of 'D'ye Ken John Peel'.

William Metcalfe (1830–1909), adaptor of the music of 'D'ye Ken John Peel'. He was a lay clerk at Carlisle Cathedral for fifty years.

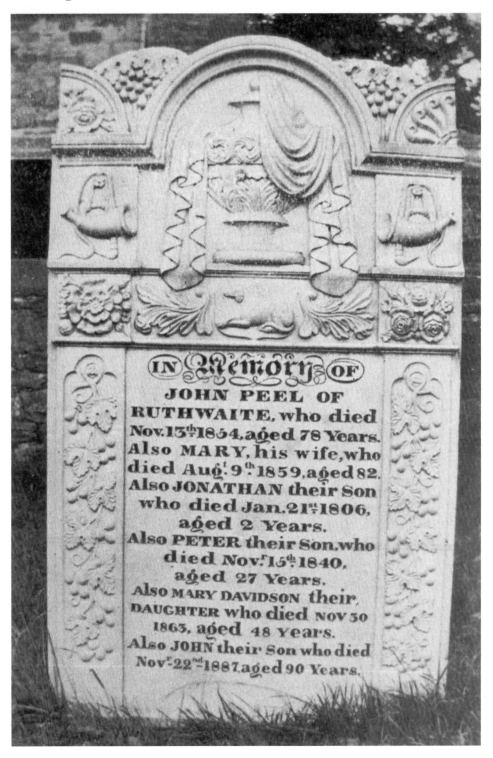

IN Memory OF
JOHN PEEL OF
RUTHWAITE, who died
Nov.13ᵗʰ1854,aged 78 Years.
Also MARY, his wife,who
died Augᵗ 9ᵗʰ1859,aged 82.
Also JONATHAN their Son
who died Jan.21ᵗ1806,
aged 2 Years.
Also PETER their Son,who
died Novʳ15ᵗʰ1840,
aged 27 Years.
Also MARY DAVIDSON their,
DAUGHTER who died NOV 30
1863, aged 48 Years.
Also JOHN their Son who died
Novʳ22ⁿᵈ1887,aged 90 Years.

John Peel's headstone, Caldbeck churchyard, visited by people from all over the world.

Miss Scoon's house at Greenrigg, which was John Peel's residence from 1777 to 1803.

Greenrigg Farm, 'back o' Skidda', was the home of this immortal huntsman; he was a striking figure, standing more than 6ft tall. He was 'treble lang in th' leg and lish (nimble), with a fine, girt (large), neb (nose), and grey eyes that could see for iver (ever).'

John Peel was a passionate fox-hunter, for which he would regularly neglect any serious business or household cares and he always hunted on foot.

He was born on 13 November 1776, had thirteen children and died on 13 November 1854, aged seventy-eight.

John Woodcock Graves, a Caldbeck wool weaver, composed the words of 'D'ye Ken John Peel' in 1832 while he was sitting by the fire with John. The tune which inspired him was an old rant called 'Bonnie Annie', which was being sung at the time by an old woman as she sang to sleep one of the Graves' own children. The setting of this old melody is due to Mr Metcalfe, choir master of Carlisle Cathedral.

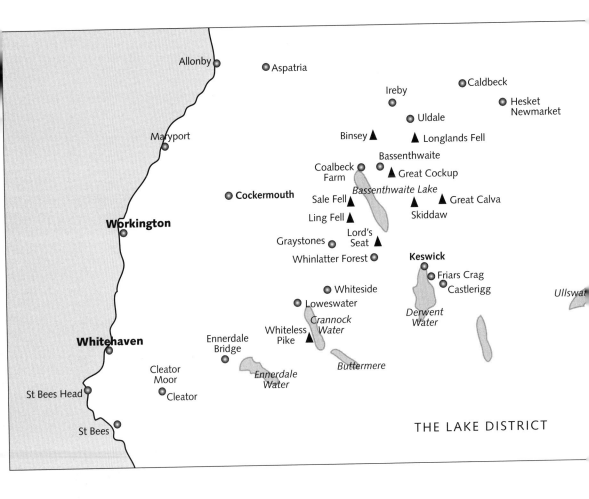

Allonby
Aspatria
Ireby
Caldbeck
Hesket Newmarket
Uldale
Maryport
Binsey ▲
▲ Longlands Fell
Bassenthwaite
Coalbeck Farm
▲ Great Cockup
Cockermouth
Sale Fell ▲
*Bassenthwaite Lake*
▲
▲ Great Calva
Ling Fell ▲
Skiddaw
Workington
Graystones
Lord's Seat ▲
Whinlatter Forest
Keswick
Friars Crag
Castlerigg
Whiteside
*Ullswat*
Loweswater
*Derwent Water*
Whitehaven
Ennerdale Bridge
Whiteless Pike ▲
*Crannock Water*
Cleator Moor
*Ennerdale Water*
*Buttermere*
St Bees Head
Cleator
St Bees

THE LAKE DISTRICT

# 2

# The Cumbrian Mountains: North-West

## ALLONBY

*OS Grid Ref: NY080432*

### 4 MILES WEST OF ASPATRIA

Allonby was once a manor on the coast some 5 miles north of Maryport. It was originally called Allan-by after the second lord of Allerdale.

Captain Jos Huddart FRS (1741–1816) was born at Allonby. He became a marine surveyor and built lighthouses and the bridges over the Eden.

Today, Allonby is a traditional Solway village that looks across the Solway Firth to the Scottish hills. To its rear lie the Lake District fells.

Smuggling was once a profitable occupation in and around Allonby and the smugglers' route trail passes close to the village. In 1730 a government enquiry into the contraband

Allonby in about 1900.

trade found that Solway people were the first working-class folk in England to drink tea regularly.

Allonby was a popular sea-bathing resort in the early 1800s. A sea water bath was built in 1835, the upper floor of which was used as a ballroom for the local nobility. It is now a Grade II listed building and stands in the old market square.

Allonby is a pleasant blend of Georgian and early Victorian charm. Its alleyways, cobbled lanes and old squares are full of character.

Allonby has a very attractive sand and shingle beach that won Seaside Awards in 1998 and 2005, and is very popular with wind-surfers. The sea fishing off Allonby is very good and the village offers excellent showjumping facilities. No wonder Allonby has become a very popular centre for holidays – day trips and longer – for many Cumbrians and for those from south-west Scotland.

## ASPATRIA                                                      *OS Grid Ref: NY145419*

### 8 MILES SOUTH-WEST OF WIGTON

The approach to Aspatria from the south is along a pleasant road that leads down a steep valley bank and crosses the River Ellen. En route some old heraldic gate posts are passed.

The old name for this mining village is Aspatrick, but it is usually referred to in the vernacular as 'Spestry'. It is a rather picturesque place that sits on the edge of a coalfield that edges West Cumbria and continues westwards under the sea. The surrounding countryside undulates and is very enjoyable.

Bullgill station, one stop west of Aspatria on the Solway Junction Railway.

Brayton station, on the Solway Junction Railway, was specially built to serve nearby Brayton Hall. It is a mile north-east of Aspatria.

Aspatria's much restored Norman church is approached through a fine avenue of yew trees. Among several ancient relics in the church are a twelfth-century intricately carved font, a Viking hog-back tombstone and a grave cover engraved with a pagan swastika. Like many other churches in the area, the churchyard contains a holy well in which it is said St Kentigern baptised his converts.

Aspatria Agricultural College adds status to the village, as does a memorial fountain to Wilfred Lawson MP (1829–1906), who was a life-long crusader for the Temperance Movement and International Peace. He was known as 'watery Wilfred' and, according to one writer, 'no man, in his day made more people laugh at Temperance meetings.'

Brayton Hall is close to Aspatria. It was bought early in the eighteenth century by the Lawsons of Isel, who remodelled it into an Italianate palace with beautiful grounds. It is now the seat of the Lawsons.

The Solway Junction Railway passed through Aspatria.

## MARYPORT                                        *OS Grid Ref: NY035365*

5 MILES NORTH-EAST OF WORKINGTON

There was a Roman cliff-top fort called Alauna where Maryport now stands; and in 1750 Maryport consisted of just two houses. One had just been built and the other one was the original Golden Lion. By 1774, it had grown to more than 100 houses

A sideways launch into a narrow channel at Maryport; a tricky business.

*Below:* An auction in progress at Maryport quay.

with 1,300 inhabitants, all attracted by the opening of the coal trade on the estate of Humphrey Senhouse, who had named the place Maryport after his wife. Other nearby mines were worked by Mr Christian of Ewanrigg and his son, John Christian Curwen MP and the Lord Lonsdale of the day. All this coal was shipped from Maryport, which grew into a considerable town with docks and a lighthouse. It faced strong competition from Whitehaven, Harrington and Workington. For a time it had considerable trade with America and exported iron as well as coal. However, its pleasant harbour was too small and it always remained a poor relation of Whitehaven. After 1899, the harbour trade declined catastrophically.

Maryport's award-winning Senhouse Roman Museum houses the largest collection of Roman altars from a single site in Britain. Other exhibits include a telescope that

Launching Maryport's new lifeboat, 27 September 1934.

belonged to mutineer Fletcher Christian of Mutiny on the *Bounty* fame, who was a local man, born at nearby Brigham. The telescope that belonged to Thomas Ismay is also housed in the museum. Ismay was a Maryport man who founded the White Star Line, owners of the ill-fated *Titanic*. The town's maritime history is reflected in the rich display of pictures, items and models in the Maritime Museum, which overlooks the harbour.

As well as becoming a busy port, Maryport developed into a shipbuilding centre where, again because of the narrowness of the channel, all the newly built ships were launched sideways. Today, the town's newly restored Georgian quayside, cliff-top path, harbour and beautiful beach attract many frequent visitors.

The artist L.S. Lowry was a frequent visitor to Maryport, where he loved painting the harbour.

## COCKERMOUTH                                           *OS GRID REF: NY125305*

### 7 MILES SOUTH-EAST OF MARYPORT

Cockermouth became a market town in 1226 and a Parliamentary borough in 1295. Its church, All Saints', was built in 1852 and Jennings Brewery was established there in the 1820s. Jennings is the last independent brewery in Cumbria. Cockermouth's Sneck Lifter deserves more than a passing glance. It is a fine Cumbrian ale, brewed by Jennings.

Cockermouth's main street is broad, lined with trees and Georgian houses and has a statue of the Earl of Mayo. He was MP for Cockermouth for ten years from 1858 before becoming Viceroy of India. This brilliant man met a sad end; he was stabbed to death by a convict at a prison settlement he was inspecting on the Andaman Islands.

William Wordsworth.

Dining room, William Wordsworth's birthplace, Cockermouth.

In the 1770s, two Cockermouth lads grew up to become the most famous of the town's sons. The elder of the two was Fletcher Christian, leader of the *Bounty* mutiny.

William Wordsworth, the younger boy, was born in 1770 at Lowther House, an elegant Georgian building at the west end of Main Street. It had been built in 1745 and William and Dorothy Wordsworth and their three brothers were all born there. The Earl of Lowther owned the house and John Wordsworth was his legal and political agent.

John Wordsworth introduced William, his son, to poetry and encouraged him to use the large family library.

The Wordsworths' garden overlooked the River Derwent and it is said that the sound of the River Derwent was William's first childhood memory.

Cockermouth has another famous son in John Dalton, the physicist, who was a member of the team to first split the atom. In recognition of his involvement in this achievement, Cockermouth's Masonic Lodge has been named John Dalton Lodge after him.

Cockermouth Castle, the seat of the Earls of Egremont, saw plenty of action against Scottish raiders; Robert the Bruce ravaged it. In 1315 during the Wars of the Roses it was attacked, and in the Civil War it was occupied by both sides in turn. Mary, Queen of Scots, took refuge there in 1568 following her defeat at the Battle of Langside. The Egremont family still lives in part of the castle, while the rest of it is open to the public during Cockermouth Festival every July.

The fine Georgian house opposite the castle entrance is Castlegate House. It was built in 1739 and exhibitions of Northern and Scottish artists are held there. At the rear of the house there is a pleasant wooded garden.

Wordsworth's house, Cockermouth.

## WORKINGTON                                            *OS Grid Ref: NY001290*

### 8 MILES WEST-SOUTH-WEST OF COCKERMOUTH

For many centuries the River Derwent has flowed through the ancient port of Workington (which began as the Roman fort of Gabrosentum), to reach the sea. Until coal mining was developed there, Workington was a tiny picturesque village where, in 1568, Mary Queen of Scots landed after her escape from Loch Leven and from where she was escorted under Queen Elizabeth's orders to Carlisle.

Before 1650 Workington was exporting coal, but by 1676 the superficial deposits had become exhausted. The Curwens resumed mining at Clifton in about 1770, about 2 miles inland from Workington, using steam pumps to reach the deeper seams. Sir James Lowther also opened a mine there and laid down a tramway to Workington's harbour; but the Lowther mines were closed suddenly in 1781. The Curwens continued and in 1800 had nine pits in operation, producing about 100,000 tons annually. In 1837, three of the pits which had been extended under the sea were flooded.

Other industries were operating in Workington at different times and the steel works of Cammel and Co. became the town's main feature. In the 1870s and 1880s, West Cumberland's iron and steel industry grew rapidly and it was broadly centred on Workington, which doubled its population in the 1860s and 1870s to about 25,000. Yet Workington never developed metal-using industries like ship-building and engineering. Resulting from this, after 1881 the population of West Cumberland remained fairly static. Today, Workington is the largest town on the Cumbrian coast.

Pow Street, Workington.

South William Street, Workington.

Workington Hall, the seat of the Curwen family for over 600 years, was built around a fourteenth-century pele tower. Over the years it was developed and extensive alterations were made to it in the nineteenth century by the then lord of the manor, John Christian Curwen, who travelled throughout Britain and Europe to research and develop a better and more profitable way of farming. His findings were adopted worldwide and are still being used today.

## HESKET NEWMARKET                              *OS Grid Ref: NY340387*

9 MILES SOUTH-EAST OF WIGTON

The 'Hesket' part of 'Hesket Newmarket' means 'racecourse' in old Scandinavian. As the other part of its name suggests, this lovely spot, set around its village green, used to have its own market, which explains why the road through the village is a wide one. The market is long gone but Hesket Newmarket is still famed for its annual sheepdog trials and agricultural show.

Once, an inn called the Queen's Head stood close to the top end of the main street and some famous folk have stayed there; Coleridge and William and Dorothy Wordsworth spent the night there on 14 August 1808. That evening, Dorothy visited nearby Caldbeck Falls. In September 1857, Charles Dickens and Wilkie Collins stayed at The Queen's Head and

Hesket Newmarket Show, 1906.

Spectators at the same Hesket
Newmarket show, 1906.

the outcome of that visit was *The Lazy Tour of Two Idle Apprentices* in which they paid this
tribute to The Queen's Head:

> What grand impressions of it those who become wanderers over the earth would carry away,
> and how at distant ends of the world some old voyagers would die, cherishing the belief
> that finest apartment known to men was once in the Hesket Newmarket Inn in rare old
> Cumberland.

When The Queen's Head closed, the building was renamed Dickens House.

Some ladies prefer a picnic and do it in style. Just look at their dresses.

Hesket Hall has a circular roof and twelve angles that serve as a sundial. It was built by Sir William Lawson, the first baronet, in 1685.

Two miles south-east of Hesket Newmarket is Haltcriff Hall, home of the Bewleys from the reign of Richard II until the reign of Charles I when the heiress brought it to the Lawsons through marriage.

## BINSEY AND IREBY                          *OS Grid Ref: NY225355*

### 1½ MILES SOUTH-WEST OF CALDBECK

Binsey, a gentle, rounded hill, occupies the north-west corner of Lakeland. At 1,466ft, it is not very high, but it is an excellent viewpoint. An ordnance survey column is sited close to the cairn that marks its summit and there is a wind-break on the summit's north side. The summit is reached from almost any direction simply by climbing a smooth, heather-clad slope. The climb is pleasant at any time of the year and you will not meet many people. This is because this pleasant climb has nothing spectacular to offer except the views from the top. To the south there is an unobstructed view of Coniston Fells, 22 miles away, and Overwater is seen to the east. To the north-west, the coasted plain is clearly seen with, beyond it, the Solway Firth. Binsey is a safe hill and an excellent introduction to the magnificence of Northern Lakeland.

High Ireby is on the northern slope of Binsey with the larger village of Ireby 1½ miles further north. Ireby has a restored market cross and a moot hall. It had a market in 1237

Thomas Victor of Martindale, aged nine, who was lost on the fells for four days and nights in July 1907. Good for him that it was summer time. He would never have got lost on Binsey.

and was an important corn market in the seventeenth century, but does not have a market today.

There are two churches at Ireby. One is a ruined Norman church and is just outside the village. The doorway is Norman, the nave has Norman arches, the chancel arch is Norman, the windows on the north and a southern one, which is blocked, and the east window are all Norman. It would have been fitting if one of the vicars had been called Norman. The other church, the one still in use, was built in 1847.

Like many Cumbrian villages, Ireby had a dancing school which was held at the Seen Inn. According to Keats, who visited the pub, the dancers 'kickit and jumpit with mettle extraordinary, tattooing the floor like mad.'

## WHITEHAVEN
*OS Grid Ref: NX978181*

### 5 MILES SOUTH OF WORKINGTON

The monks of nearby St Bees Priory were using Whitehaven as a harbour before the twelfth century. Following the Reformation, the Lowther family acquired the land and developed it to enable them to expand their coal industry. At a time when growth along Cumbria's coastal area was slow, Whitehaven mushroomed from a hamlet of just six thatched cottages in 1633 to a sizeable town. By 1693 the population of Whitehaven was 2,000. The town had been planned to a grid system, unusual in Cumbria. Great care was taken in expanding Whitehaven which now boasts 250 listed buildings. By the mid-eighteenth century it had become the third largest port in Britain. Coal was the main export and imports included tobacco from Virginia.

Many emigrants to the New World sailed from Whitehaven. With the advent of steam, Whitehaven's shallow harbour could not accommodate the large iron steam ships and lost out to places like Southampton and Liverpool. Whitehaven Harbour has changed little since those days. The harbour and its environs have been declared a conservation area.

Whitehaven has a museum that looks like a small lighthouse and in it the history of the town and the harbour is brought to life through modern display methods. The museum is called The Beacon.

In the 1770s, William and Dorothy Wordsworth stayed at Whitehaven as children and were fascinated by the town, the harbour and the white waves breaking against its quays and piers.

Bransty Arch,
Whithaven.

Whitehaven's
open market.

Whitehaven
Castle from the
road.

In 1778, during the American War of Independence, John Paul Jones, the American. privateer, sailed into Whitehaven Harbour and planted incendiary devices in a number of ships at the quay. He did so at dead of night. The resulting fires were quenched and Jones was driven away by gunfire from the harbour batteries. Whitehaven holds the honour of being the last English fort to have been attacked by American warships.

## St Bees Head                                   *OS Grid Ref: NX943133*

### 3 MILES SOUTH OF WHITEHAVEN

St Bees Head overlooks the Irish Sea almost a mile south-east of North Head, which is the furthest west that Cumbria stretches. It is a red sandstone bluff some 4 miles long and 300ft high. It forms one of the most dramatic natural features along the full coastline of north-west England. Looking out to sea from St Bees Head, dark shadows that are the Isle of Man and the Irish coast can be seen on a clear day. Alfred Wainwright's Coast to Coast walk starts at St Bees and goes westwards to St Bees Head before heading eastwards.

Once, St Bees Head had a beacon which guided passing ships away from the rocks. It was replaced by a lighthouse in 1822 but the lighthouse was destroyed by fire and the present one replaced it in 1867.

St Bees Head is a very important Nature Reserve. Guillemots, gulls, razorbills, kittiwakes, skuas and gannets crowd the cliffs. The RSPB provides twitchers - bird watchers – with observation and information points along the headland.

Also at St Bees Head are lots of caravans, but they blend in reasonably well.

St Bees Head, almost as far west as Northern Lakeland gets.

The main street, St Bees, in about 1900.

A footpath goes along the coast from St Bees to Whitehaven. It passes Saltam Pit, which was the world's first under-sea mine shaft.

St Bees and St Bees Head are thought to have been named after the nunnery of St Bega who was an Irish noblewoman who fled to Cumbria to escape an undesirable marriage. She asked the local lord for some land for a nunnery and was told that she could have as much land as could be covered by snow on midsummer's day. It did, in fact, snow on midsummer's day, so she got her land. The Benedictine nunnery was founded in about AD 650. It was later destroyed by sea raider, but the Normans founded a priory on the same spot in the twelfth century.

## CLEATOR AND CLEATOR MOOR  *OS Grid Ref: NY018410*

### 2 MILES SOUTH-EAST OF WHITEHAVEN

Cleator and Cleator Moor are both derived from the Norse words for cliff and hill pasture. Both places are old villages that expanded in the boom of iron ore mining during the nineteenth century when the demand for coal and iron ore was insatiable. The Cumbrian poet, Norman Nicholson, succinctly encapsulated the situation when he wrote:

> From one shaft at Cleator Moor
> They mined for coal and iron ore.
> This harvest below ground could show
> Black and red currants on one tree.

By 1842, the Whitehaven Haematite Iron Company had two blast furnaces operating to the west of Cleator Moor. There were four main mines in the vicinity and the ore produced was of the highest quality. Henry Bessemer, who invented a method of producing cheaper steel from pig iron, relied entirely on haematite iron made at Cleator Moor and Workington. A third of all the output of Cumbrian haematite was produced at Cleator Moor.

By the end of the nineteenth century both the iron ore and the coal mines were almost worked out. The red dust created by the iron industry gradually cleared and both Cleator and Cleator Moor residents were able to breath clean air once again.

Fletcher Town, a West Cumbrian mining village similar to Cleator.

A Methodist Chapel, built in Lakeland style.

Today there is little evidence of the area's industrial past. The surrounding countryside is very pleasant and there is a large factory shop in Cleator village that stocks a huge range of outdoor clothing, caps, bags, scarves, golf wear and the like. That, surely, must be a step in the right direction.

## ENNERDALE BRIDGE AND ENNERDALE WATER     *OS Grid Ref: NY073161*

7 MILES EAST OF WHITEHAVEN

The River Ehen flows westwards out of Ennerdale Water, one of the most secluded and inaccessible of all the lakes in Northern Lakeland. Some 2 miles downstream from where it leaves Ennerdale Water, the River Ehen is crossed by a minor road at Ennerdale Bridge, a hamlet of neat cottages that give a touch of character to this pleasant place. It is sited just inside the National Park boundary. When William Wordsworth wrote about Ennerdale Bridge in 'The Brothers' he described its shaded churchyard as being 'girt around with a bare ring of mossy wall.' It still is.

Ennerdale Bridge was chosen by the renowned fell walker, Alfred Wainwright, as the first overnight stopping place on his coast to coast walk when tackled from west to east. It is a good base from which to explore Ennerdale Water, although walkers with cars can take advantage of the two car parks at the western end of the lake. There is a third car park at Bowness Knott, midway along the north shore.

Ennerdale Water, much loved by seekers of solitude.

During the summer months, Bowness Knott is the terminus of the 'Ennerdale Rambler' bus, which runs from Cockermouth, Buttermere and Loweswater. Cars can go no further than Bowness Knott, though there is access for vehicles to Ennerdale YHA and to a couple of nearby picnic areas.

Ennerdale Water, the most westerly of the lakes, is in a remote but pleasantly rural setting. It is famed as a fishery for brown trout and char. It supplies water to South Cumbria Water Board.

Once the upper part of Ennerdale was a rocky wilderness, devoid of trees. Then the Forestry Commission changed the landscape by planting great numbers of trees, mixing vast amounts of broad-leaved varieties with conifers. These were not planted in straight lines, as used to be the case, but following contours. This has softened the landscape and provided fine footpaths, but Ennerdale remains virtually untouched.

## BUTTERMERE AND WHITELESS PIKE $\qquad$ *OS Grid Ref: NY180189*

BUTTERMERE 5 MILES SOUTH-WEST OF KESWICK

Buttermere is a delightful little lake that has a lot to offer. To walk around it is an absolute joy. There are only a few yards of road-walking and the views throughout are superb. Buttermere means 'the lake by the dairy pastures' and it is very fitting. A walk around Buttermere will give you some exciting views of Fleetwith Pike, 1½ miles to the south-east. Walking around Buttermere, which is only 1½ miles long and just under ½ a mile wide, will take you a little over two hours. As you walk clockwise along the north shore, you will enter a short tunnel. The story goes that a local landowner was annoyed because he could not walk all the way around the lake because of a rocky barrier, so he blasted a way through the rock. Now everyone can walk around Buttermere with little effort. The National Trust owns the lake and hires out rowing boats.

Buttermere, Red Pike and High Stile.

*Top left:* Crummock Water, Buttermere's next-door neighbour. Both lakes are renowned for their solitude.

*Centre:* Buttermere Valley. At one time Buttermere and Crummock Water were one lake.

*Left:* The solitude of Crummock Water. It has a Celtic name, is 144ft deep, 2½ miles long and just over ½ a mile wide. A narrow strip of land ½ a mile long separates it from Buttermere.

*Above:* Lakeland visitors coaching up Buttermere.

Beautiful Buttermere, half the size of its neighbour, Crummock Water, is thought by many to be the most splendid of all the lakes. From it there are superb views of the eastern towers of Fleetwith Pikes and the great line-up of High Crag, High Stile and Red Pike.

From the road near Rannerdale Farm, just over a mile west of Buttermere village, Whiteless Pike, at 2,159ft, looks like most people's conception of a mountain, a pyramid shape with uniform sides and a small peak for a summit. However, looked at from any other angle and the triangular outline is not maintained.

The summit of Whiteless Pike is tiny and has a cluster of stones, like a collapsed cairn, at its highest point. It is a superb viewing point.

A popular way to reach this viewpoint is from Buttermere up Whiteless Breast. There is a clear path which is followed all the way to the top and from mid-way up there is a good view of Causey Pike in the distance.

Squat Beck flows down Whiteless Pike and several feeders join it. Many of these feeders vanish underground at about the 700ft contour. If feeders could see, they would stay on the surface because the whole area is spectacular.

## WHITESIDE AND WHINLATTER FOREST          *OS Grid Ref: NY170220*

### 2 MILES EAST OF LOWESWATER

Heading south along the Vale of Lorton towards Crummock Water, the vast mass of Brackenthwaite Fell looms on the left. It is a magnificent site – nature in the raw. It is a place to be treated with respect. Here the buttresses of Whiteside climb out of the valley blocking the expected view of Buttermere Lake and the Southern Lakeland mountains, among them Scafell Pike and Bow Fell, the highest land in England. Whiteside is 2,317ft high and has three buttresses on its western side. They are Whiteside End, Dodd and Penn. Together they tower steeply from the flattish Cumbrian plain. They are tough and craggy and, collectively, form a rough bulky cornerstone of fell that is very dramatic. The top of Whiteside is narrow and grassy. In a short distance an exciting view down Gasdale Gill opens up before you. Gasdale Beck runs along the bottom of Gasdale Gill, east to west.

Braithwaite village is set in exceptional scenery on the edge of Whinlatter Forest Park, the only mountain forest in England. From its Dodd Wood viewing point it is possible to see ospreys through high-powered binoculars.

Near the head of Gasdale Gill, Gasdale Beck tumbles over some very spectacular waterfalls.

Two miles north-east of Whiteside an unclassified road climbs through Whinlatter Forest Park using Whinlatter Pass. Moving from east to west along Whinlatter Pass, at first there is forest on both sides, then only on the left, then only on the right. This is Whinlatter Forest.

Whinlatter is one of only two National Forest Parks in the whole of Lakeland. Both are predominantly broad-leaved, semi-natural woodlands and are regarded as two of Lakeland's most valuable scenic wildlife assets.

Whinlatter Pass is the easiest of all the Lakeland passes although there are some steep sections.

## GRAYSTONES AND WHINLATTER                    *OS Grid Ref: NY177265*

### 5 MILES SOUTH-EAST OF COCKERMOUTH

Graystones at 1,476ft is not a mountain or a fell. It is the highest point of a fell called Kirk Fell, which is reached using steeply-rising ground northwards from Whinlatter Pass and keeping close to woodland on the right.

Continue northwards beyond Graystones and the land falls away rather more gently across Wythrop Moss. The infant Tom Rudd Beck begins here and descends to join up with another branch in front of steep-sided, conical Ling Fell. The beck now flows westwards, curving right to go round Ling Fell before continuing northwards. The land north of Ling Fell changes into rough pasture, which descends into Embleton valley. The land to the west of Graystones descends in similar fashion to the flat valley bottom of the River Cocker.

One mile south-east of Graystones is Brown How, the summit of 1,696ft high Whinlatter, which is a lonely fell, frequented by sheep. Its steep, south-facing slopes are carpeted with bracken and is streaked with scree. Whinlatter Fell is surrounded by Thornthwaite afforestation in various degrees of thickness. Whinlatter Pass runs east to west about a quarter of a mile south of the summit of Whinlatter Fell, at the foot of a steep declivity.

Whinlatter is one of those fells considered too rough for many hikers to tackle, yet once the climb is done, the ridge reached is completely different and is a pleasure to behold. Now a forest road through Hospital Plantation can be used. This is the least difficult way up. How now, Brown How!

'Devils Elbow' coaches returning from Buttermere to Keswick.

# Ling Fell and Lord's Seat

*OS Grid Ref: NY180285*

### 4 MILES SOUTH-EAST OF COCKERMOUTH

At 1,224ft in height, Ling Fell is not a very tall Northern Lakeland fell. It is not particularly attractive either. It is an isolated, rounded hill with lots of heather on its sides. It has a broad top on which there is a mix of grass, heather, gorse and bracken. An Ordnance Survey trig point marks the summit of the dome-shaped fell and from it the Skiddaw group of mountains to the east can be seen.

Four miles distant, Cockermouth is seen to the north-west. Ling Fell, which rises out of Wythop Moss, is dwarfed by Lord's Seat, 2 miles to the south-east, which is 1,811ft high. With Thornthwaite Forest below it, immediately to the south-east, and Wythop Wood to the north-east and edging Bassenthwaite Lake, Lord's Seat, with its superior height, holds a commanding position that suits its name. Lord's Seat has four ridges that radiate from its summit. All four ridges enclose streams that flow north, south, east and west, and all four becks meet in the River Derwent. The Forestry Commission has, over many years, planted lots of conifers, mainly spruces. On two of Lord's Seat's ridges, the elevation of Barf and Seat How are excellent view points. They overlook the Vale of Keswick, south of Lord's Seat. Thornthwaite Forest, planted by the Forestry Commission, spreads south for 2 miles and is more than a mile wide. North of Lord's Seat another Forestry Commission-developed forest, Wythop Wood, which spreads for 3 miles, edging Bassenthwaite Lake for most of the way. Lord's Seat is the geographical centre of all Forestry Commission activities south of Bassenthwaite Lake and there are plantations on all sides.

# Sale Fell and Wythop Valley

*OS Grid Ref: NY195297*

### 4 MILES EAST-SOUTH-EAST OF COCKERMOUTH

Sale Fell is the furthest north of the North Western Fells. It is 1,170ft high and the views from its summit range across the Cumbrian Plain to the Scottish coast. Sale Fell marks the top end of Lakeland. It is grassy with a good carpet of bracken and from it there are good views of Wythop Valley and as far as Skiddaw beyond it. The wooded eastern slopes of Sale Fell are within the boundaries of an old part of Thornthwaite Forest known as Wythop Wood, which is a mix of deciduous trees and evergreens.

The Pheasant Inn is at the foot of Sale Fell, close to Bassenthwaite Lake. The pub is so named because, at one time, the surrounding area was a centre for the rearing of game birds.

Beautiful roe deer, very shy creatures, frequent Wythop Wood. They are free to roam in the older woodland around Sale Fell but cannot get into the new plantations.

The Wythop Valley lies between Sale Fell and Ling Fell and its entrance at Wythop Mill is narrow and so enclosed with trees that it could easily be missed. Wythop Valley is an unspoiled, quiet place and a scenic farming area, hidden away from Lakeland tourists. Wythop Beck flows from the steep northern slope of Broom Fell westwards along Wythop

Sale Fell drops steeply through Wythop Woods to Bassenthwaite Lake. The next nearest lake is Crummock Water, pictured here, 6 miles away to the south-west.

The village 6 miles north of Sale Fell and pictured here, is Bothal. The name is derived from Bo-hill, meaning 'beacon on the hill'.

Valley, at the eastern end of which it passes Wythop Hall. The original Wythop Hall was fortified and built by the Lowthers in 1319. The present building was constructed by the Fletchers in the seventeenth century.

Locals call Wythop Valley 'With-up' and Wainwright calls it a geographical freak 'because it is not moulded at all to the usual pattern.'

## BASSENTHWAITE LAKE                    *OS Grid Ref: NY220300*

### 2½ MILES NORTH-WEST OF KESWICK

Bassenthwaite Lake is the only lake in the Lake District; all the others are waters or meres. It is also the most northerly of all the Lakeland lakes. Bass Lake, as it is affectionately called by Cumbrians, is 4 miles long and ¾ of a mile wide but only 70ft deep. It is edged with vegetation, which makes it an ideal habitat for birds; more than seventy species of which have been recorded there. Bassenthwaite Lake is a Nature Reserve, owned by

Bassenthwaite Lake, the only lake in the Lake District.

The Pheasant Hotel, a hostelry of renown, at the northern end of Wythop Wood, overlooking Bassenthwaite Lake.

Bassenthwaite Lake from Whinlatter.

Out for a drive in
the Lakes, 1920.
The A66 edges
Bassenthwaite
Lake.

the National Park Authority and parts of it are out of bounds to boats of any kind. This
encourages bird life, which improves the richness of the area.

To the east of Bassenthwaite Lake, the great bulk of Skiddaw towers.

Water, flowing north from Derwent Water along the River Derwent, feeds
Bassenthwaite Lake. At one time Bassenthwaite Lake and Derwent Water were one lake.
These days, following heavy, prolonged rain they almost become one again.

Near The Pheasant, close to the north-west corner of Bassenthwaite Lake, a craggy,
whitewashed rock overlooks the A66, which runs along the edge of the lake before
turning west to Cockermouth. Legend has it that a bishop tried to ride his horse up the
scree-covered fellside behind The Pheasant to demonstrate his faith in God to get him
to the top. His faith was unfounded. The climb was so steep that the horse overbalanced
backwards, throwing the bishop off its back. Both of them fell to the foot of the scree
and were killed. By tradition the rock from which they fell is kept whitewashed by the
landlord of The Pheasant.

The first regatta to be held on a Cumbrian lake took place at Bassenthwaite Lake on
24 August 1780.

To Wordsworth, Bassenthwaite Lake was mysterious. He called it Broad water.

## BINSEY AND COALBECK FARM          *OS Grid Ref: NY226355*

### 1½ MILES SOUTH-EAST OF ULDALE

Binsey is a solitary, gentle hill that stands apart from the main mass of the other fells of
Northern Lakeland. It is not a very high hill, reaching only 1,466ft; that will break no
records for height in Northern Lakeland! However, it is a safe place, full of gentle slopes
and without pitfalls. Binsey comes into its own as a view point. From its summit the fells
of Northern Lakeland can be assessed and the views it offers are superb.

Delightful kittens like Darby and Joan introduce children to Northern Lakeland's wonderful world of nature.

*400 Darby & Joan*

The rocks of all the neighbouring fells are slate but the Binsey rocks are volcanic. Binsey is sited at the north-west of Northern Lakeland, 2 miles north-east of Bassenthwaite Lake. The coastal plain of Cumbria is clearly seen north of Binsey, with the Solway Firth and Scotland beyond.

On the northern shore of Bassenthwaite Lake there are some signs that direct you to Trotters World of Animals at Coalbeck Farm. It is home to hundreds of animals and is a wonderful place for children because they are encouraged to feed them. There are even harmless snakes that children are allowed to handle. There are birds of prey displays, tractor and pony rides and a play area. For many children who think that chickens come from supermarkets, Trotters World of Animals is an eye-opener.

Coalbeck Farm is open to the public from mid-February to October, 10 a.m. to 5.30 p.m. and from mid-November to mid February, 11 a.m. to 4.30 p.m. Trotters can cater for school groups either for an informal day out or for a structured programme based on National Curriculum requirements.

## LONGLANDS FELL AND BRAE FELL

*OS Grid Ref: NY275354*

LONGLANDS FELL, 2 MILES SOUTH-EAST OF ULDALE

Longlands Fell is 1,580ft tall and is situated at the end of the north-west ridge of Great Scafell. It marks the furthest point that the Lakeland fells spread in a north-westerly direction. It is a neat pyramid of a hill and is conspicuous despite being dominated by the bulkier masses of Lowthwaite Fell and Brae Fell. The village of Longlands is tucked into the north-west foot of Longlands Fell, 1 mile north-east of Overwater Tarn.

Overwater is a Norse name and is on the very edge of the Lake District. A dam has been placed across its northern end, enlarging it and turning it into a reservoir for Wigton. In 1992 it was handed over to the National Trust.

Motoring in lake country is very exciting as this picture of motoring up Buttermere Hause shows; scenes like this are common throughout Lakeland.

Brae Fell is a grassy fell, 1,920ft high with a fine cairn on its summit. The cairn was built of stones that had been scattered around the summit before man came on the scene; a rare occasion where nature scatters its rubbish and man tidies up after it.

As sometimes happens in Northern Lakeland – and Southern Lakeland too – a dreary climb to the summit of a fell is rewarded with a brilliant view. Both Longlands Fell and Brae Fell are examples of this.

From Brae Fell the view eastwards, across the Eden Valley, is superb. It is one of the best among the northern fells.

The 70-mile-long Cumbrian Way, which starts at Ulverston on Morecambe Bay and goes right through the heart of the Lake District, skirts both Longlands Fell and Brae Fell. The journey it takes is a rather exciting one.

## Skiddaw House, Whitewater Dash and Great Calva
*OS Grid Ref: NY288292*

### 3 MILES EAST-NORTH-EAST OF BASSENTHWAITE VILLAGE

Skiddaw House, which is backed by trees, was built as a shooting lodge. Later, it became a shepherd's 'bothy' and now it is the highest youth hostel in Britain. It was at Skiddaw House that Hugh Walpole's famous duel took place between Uhland and John Herries in *The Fortress*. Hugh Walpole also used Skiddaw House as the model for Green House in his novel *The Bright Pavilions*.

A track leads from Skiddaw House to a waterfall 2 miles away, called Whitewater Dash, situated on the west side of Little Calva. Both Little Calva (2,110ft), and Great Calva (2,265ft), lie side by side in Skiddaw Forest. In 1800, Samuel Coleridge visited Whitewater Dash waterfall and noted its complexity, 'parts rushing in wheels, other parts perpendicular, some in white horse tails, they are the finest water furies I ever beheld.'

Skiddaw Forest does not lend itself to villages with an open aspect like Tallentire, pictured here. Such villages are usually found in flattish places like the Cumbrian Plain.

When approached along the path from Skiddaw House, Great Calva's pyramid shape looks splendid, thrusting to the sky. It rises from Skiddaw Forest, its lower slopes covered in deep heather. A beck that develops into the River Caldew is met and crossed on a footbridge at the foot of Great Calva, about ½ a mile after leaving Skiddaw House.

Once across the footbridge, Great Calva rises steeply. The going is hard and when the cairn ahead is clearly seen, it is cause to have a breather before the final plod to it. On reaching the cairn, the realisation that it does not mark the summit becomes obvious. There are a further 150 yards of gentle climb still to go.

A vast geological fault runs north to south through Lakeland. Thirlmere, Grasmere, Rydale Water and Windermere all lie in this fault. From the northern end, Great Calva looks right along the fault offering superb views.

## GREAT COCKUP AND BAKESTALL                    *OS Grid Ref: NY275334*

### 3 MILES NORTH-EAST OF BASSENTHWAITE VILLAGE

Anyone with a liking for deep bracken will like Great Cockup. It is 1,720ft high, looks dark and patchy where the bracken has been burned off, and doesn't appear to have much of a summit. Great Cockup is not a Northern Lakeland fell with a capacity to make you drool; but it serves a very useful purpose. Its long, thin spine, rising steeply from Orthwaite, acts as a barrier between the River Ellen and the feeders of the River Derwent.

It was at the popping stone, Gillsland, pictured here that Sir Walter Scott popped the question to his young lady, Miss Carpenter. She said 'yes' and later they were married in St Mary's Church, Carlisle Cathedral. It is a scene reminiscent of Skiddaw Forest.

Farm ladies at Applethwaite village, 1900, going to do the the milking.

To the north-east, Great Cockup ends abruptly, dropping steeply into the narrow Dash Valley, short of the heights of Meal Fell at 1,770ft. Westwards the land descends, then rises to Little Cockup before descending to Orthwaite village.

As the bulk of Skiddaw thrusts northwards through Skiddaw Forest, it reaches a natural feature called Bakestall. This feature is a summit, not a fell, and it is sited above and to the south of Dead Crags. A large section of the north side of Bakestall has broken away from the main mass of fell, leaving a steep exposed area of rock and scree.

The road to Skiddaw House contours the foot of Dead Crags and at their eastern end, edges Dash Beck, close to where the beck tumbles over Dash Falls, one of the most spectacular waterfalls in Northern Lakeland. Here the water plunges through a series of spectacular cataracts which, in spate, is a fearsome sight. This is visual proof that nature must always be treated with due respect.

The summit cairn of Bakestall stands about 100 yards north of the summit itself, overlooking the Dash Valley.

From the cairn, the view southwards is somewhat restricted by Skiddaw itself. However, looking to the north-west there is a good view to the Solway and the Scottish hills beyond.

## SKIDDAW: HIGH MAN                    *OS Grid Ref: NY264291*

### 3 MILES NORTH OF KESWICK

Skiddaw, at 3,053ft, is the highest mountain in Northern Lakeland. There are only three peaks in the whole of Lakeland higher than Skiddaw. Yet despite its height, it is perfectly safe, even in mist or darkness. This gentle mountain has no dangerous precipices or rugged outcrops. Skiddaw is composed of slate, which is a sedimentary rock, the oldest kind of rock in the Lake District. Unlike hard, volcanic rock, slate breaks easily into fragments and this gives Skiddaw its even terrain.

A ring of lesser peaks surrounds the summit of Skiddaw, all being part of the Skiddaw group of mountains. Together they provide a good example of how mountain groups are formed.

Because Skiddaw looks larger than it really is, this has given rise to the following expression, which is not true:

Skiddaw, Lanwellin (Helvellyn) and Casticand (Castye Carn)
Are the highest hills in all England.

Skiddaw dominates Northern Lakeland and the people who live to the north of it describe themselves as living 'back o' Skiddaw'.

Skiddaw was the first popular mountain climb in Lakeland and the broad, eroded path up its steep, grassy slope from Keswick has been used by millions of people over the years. Although there are several routes up Skiddaw, the one from Keswick is the most popular. From it are excellent views, looking backwards, over Keswick and Derwent Water.

Derwent Water and Skiddaw from Ashness Bridge.

Armathwaite Hall Hotel, near Keswick and Skiddaw.

Skiddaw's main ridge forms a watershed between the River Derwent and the River Caldew, which is a feeder of the River Eden and runs into it at Carlisle. This gentle mountain also protects Keswick from the worst of the northerly weather.

For anyone on the summit of Skiddaw with doubts about how to descend from it, just follow the crowd.

# SKIDDAW: LITTLE MAN                          *OS Grid Ref: NY266291*

## 1 MILE SOUTH-SOUTH-EAST OF SKIDDAW HIGH MAN

Skiddaw Little Man is 2,837ft high and commands an absolutely splendid, panoramic view of the very heart of the Lake District. It is a very distinctive, peaked summit with independent routes to the top; and it has two names: on ordnance survey maps it is called Little Man while Bartholomew's maps show it as Low Man.

In general, the higher you go up a fell, the better the view. The one from Skiddaw High Man takes in about four-fifths of the fells in the district, including those visible from Castlehead and Latrigg. Nevertheless, as the panorama gains in extent, it loses in beauty. The view from Little Man is superior to that from High Man.

Like its big brother High Man, Little Man is made of Skiddaw slate and this accounts for its fairly even terrain. Its name was given to it because it is overshadowed by High Man; however, this does not take into account the mountain's stature – Little Man rises ½ a mile above Bassenthwaite Lake and is anything but little.

Together, Skiddaw High Man, Little Man and Lonscale Fell form the watershed between the Rivers Derwent and Eden catchment areas; and this is more evident on the clearly defined slopes of Little Man than on the broader slopes of Skiddaw itself. Of these three summits, Little Man is the only one to feed the River Eden, which it does along the River Caldew.

Because the summit of Little Man is only about 200ft lower than that of High Man, the two together are seen by poets as the equivalent of Mount Parnassus, classical source of poetic inspiration and famously 'two-headed' in Greek poetry.

Skiddaw from the shores of Derwent Water.

Skiddaw and Keswick from Brandelhow Park.

## GEORGE SMITH, THE SKIDDAW HERMIT

Although he is best known as a Cumbrian character, George Smith was a Scot, born in Banffshire. He gained fame as the 'Skiddaw Hermit' because he lived alone in a human-sized bird's nest, perched on a ledge of Skiddaw Dodd. His 'nest' really did look exactly like that of a bird. It was large enough for him to get into through a large hole at the top, through which he would ease himself, having climbed up a nearby wall. Inside his 'nest' he had a stone for a table and a bed made of leaves; and this was where he lived come rain or shine.

George was a hardy individual. He wore neither a hat, coat or shoes. He washed his shirt in a beck and dried it on his back. He frequently ate his meat and potatoes raw and was especially fond of whisky. So fond was he, in fact, of a drop or two of the hard stuff that he often found himself in the hands of the local police. George did a bit of painting, mostly portraits, for which he refused payment; and he was thought to have 'religious mania'.

Mr George Smith, the 'Skiddaw Hermit'. This is believed to be the only picture of him ever taken.

To most of the people of Keswick, George was part of the landscape, a harmless addition to the area's interests. For the most part he never bothered with anyone and nobody bothered him. Even when he had overindulged in the hard stuff, the local police knew how to deal with him.

One day, some people, thought to be visitors to Keswick, attacked his 'nest' home and destroyed it. Poor George was devastated. The authorities found accommodation for him in Keswick. After a while he was removed to an asylum in Banffshire, and that was the last anyone heard of the 'Skiddaw Hermit'.

## KESWICK                                            *OS Grid Ref: NY260233*

Little is certain about the Roman settlement in the Keswick neighbourhood. If they had a camp there, all traces of it have now gone. In about AD 550, after the Romans had gone, St Kentigern came to the mountains now known as Skiddaw from Carlisle to preach to the half-savage and heathen hill folk. He set up a cross in a thick wood called Crossfield where, in about 1180, a church was built and dedicated to him.

Mining for plumbago or graphite, copper and lead had been carried out in the Keswick area since before the reign of Henry III by English miners. In 1564 Queen Elizabeth I brought German miners to Cumberland to look for ore using techniques that were far more advanced than those of the English. The Germans settled in the Keswick area, sank new mines and made great profits.

Main Street and Moot Hall, Keswick.

Greta Bridge, Keswick.

Keswick, pictured here in 1903.

Edward I gave Keswick its market charter. This, with its mining population, old woollen industries like those at Kendal and, a little later on, the manufacture of pencils, helped to make it something of a business place. At the end of the eighteenth century and in the early nineteenth century, pencils were made by hand from the famous Borrowdale 'wad' and 'black canke' or black lead from the mine near Seathwaite.

When tourists were first discovering the beauties of the lakes, the leading figure in Keswick was Peter Crosthwaite (1735–1808), a local man. He opened a museum in The Square in 1790, which was a great attraction until its dispersion in 1870. Today there are several fine museums in and around Keswick including Keswick Museum and Art Gallery and Fitz Park. One of Northern Lakeland's oddest museums (more a collection of strange objects than a museum), is Cars of the Stars Museum, which holds a collection of thirty vehicles which have appeared in TV and films, including such gems as Laurel and Hardy's Model T Ford. Also present is Cumberland Pencil Museum which boasts a pencil that is 6ft long, the largest pencil in the world.

Tourism is Keswick's major industry today. This is not surprising because it is the largest town in the Lake District National Park. It developed along the banks of the River Greta, is built of local stone and has a wide main street. Its attractive Moot Hall houses tourist information centres for the town and the National Park. Keswick sits at the foot of Skiddaw, close to Bassenthwaite Lake and closer still to Derwent Water, which gives it a setting that is stunningly beautiful; all the attributes of a tourist centre are there.

## KESWICK CONVENTION

Keswick becomes home to Keswick Convention for a fortnight every July. During that time, evangelical Christians from near and far gather there for meetings and services.

Keswick Convention came into being in 1875 when Canon Battersby of St John's Church, Keswick, thought of the idea of bringing together all denominations for worship. He was supported by Robert Wilson, a Cockermouth businessman, who was a Quaker. The first Keswick Convention was held in a tent in the vicarage garden and lasted for three days. So successful was it that during the next few years so many people wanted to attend Keswick Convention that special trains had to be brought into service to deal with them. Today, special trains are not required but the event stills pulls in the crowds.

When Wilfred Owen, the English poet, attended the convention in 1912, he stayed in a camp about 1½ miles from Keswick. He described his tent as having three beds, 'each equipped with one blanket (of stuff like sackcloth).' He did not like the food, which he

Convention Tent, Skiddaw Street, Keswick, 1907.

Worshippers at Keswick Convention, 1907.

called 'very ordinary indeed' and the tea was 'horrid'. He did not think much of the preaching either.

There were times during the fortnight of Keswick Convention when the tendency to get everyone to pray, irrespective of where they were, seemed to be a bit over the top. Many pedestrians did not take kindly to being asked to pray on the pavement; when they were stopped many felt embarrassed about it. But the people of Keswick have come to expect that sort of thing during the fortnight of the convention.

## CASTLERIGG STONE CIRCLE                    *OS Grid Ref: NY286227*

### 1½ MILES SOUTH-EAST OF KESWICK

Castlerigg stone circle is sited on a plateau near Keswick. It is dwarfed by encroaching fells and is believed to date from 3,000 BC; this makes it older than Stonehenge. It is thought to be the finest stone circle in England and one of the oldest in Europe. Castlerigg stone circle is approximately 98ft by 157ft, so it is not quite circular. Its circumference is made of forty-eight Borrowdale volcanic stones, the largest of which is almost 8ft tall. There is an oblong chamber inside the stone circle on the east side, but no one knows why it is there.

Castlerigg stone circle probably had an astronomical or timekeeping function when erected, but no one really knows. The entrance to the circle is at due north. Although it has been shown on early maps as a Druid circle, it dates from Late Neolithic to Early Bronze Age, long before the Druids appeared on the scene. There are other stone circles on the

Castlerigg stone circle near Keswick.

A more general view of Castlerigg stone circle.

verge of Cumbria where there was good agricultural land, places like the Cumbrian Plain, the coast and the Eden Valley. However, Castlerigg stone circle is situated right in the middle of a ring of fells. It has been calculated that the view from Castlerigg stone circle takes in all the high peaks in a circle 527ft in circumference. It is thought that the site must have been chosen with care and that the circle had astronomical meaning with the stones aligned to the stars and the sun. Other stones are thought to have been inside the circle; but these have been lost. Thousands of years ago, stars had a religious meaning, so the stone circle probably once had a religious connotation. Whatever its true origins, Castlerigg stone circle captivates the mood of the surrounding fells. Keats saw it on a bad day as:

> A dismal cirque
> of Druid stones upon a forlorn moor.

# Bass Village to Ullock Pike
*OS Grid Ref: NY243288*

### 1 MILE WEST OF SKIDDAW

The Lake District National Park is famed for its spectacular walks, many of which are in Northern Lakeland. The one from Bass village along the Edge to 3½-mile-distant Ullock Pike, at 2,230ft, is such a walk.

Bassenthwaite village – Bass village as it is known except on OS maps – is a pleasant place from which to start the walk.

Leave the village going south, along a minor road, and at once, where it bifurcates, take the right fork, going south. On reaching a major road at Chapel, turn left along it, soon to curve right. Where a minor road on the left meets the main road at a tangent, turn left along it. In a few yards at the top of the rise, turn right through a gate in a recess in a hedge on the right and follow a zig-zag green track that soon swings to the left, going through three gates to reach open fell beyond an intake wall at the narrow entrance to Southerndale. Continue up steeply rising ground that leads straight to the Edge. Close to where The Edge is joined, a cluster of rocky outcrops that have pushed through the grass, is passed on the right, close to the ridge top. They are called, enigmatically, The Watches. The Edge separates Southerndale from Bass Lake and the walk along the top, always good, improves as height is gained and Ullock Pike is approached. The Edge is curved like a bow with Ullock Pike at its southern end. The Edge is thrilling to walk along, with excellent all round views. From Ullock Pike the best view is of Bassenthwaite Lake.

Northern Lakeland's fox-hunting country spreads far beyond Bassenthwaite village and Ullock Pike across all Cumbria and beyond. Here C. N. Barry, master and huntsman, of the Caldbeck foxhounds is pictured hunting on the fells.

# FRIAR'S CRAG
*OS Grid Ref: NY265222*

### ON THE SOUTH SIDE OF KESWICK

Friar's Crag is a wooded peninsula at the northern end of Derwent Water. It was from Friar's Crag that medieval pilgrims sailed to St Herbert's Island in the middle of Derwent Water to seek the hermit's blessing. Friar's Crag is dedicated to the memory of Canon Rawnsley, a local vicar who was one of the founders of the National Trust, which he helped to set up in 1895. The National Trust bought Friar's Crag in 1922 and it has long been a beauty spot.

Arthur Ransome based Darien in *Swallows and Amazons* on Friar's Crag, which 'dropped like a cliff into the lake.' .

There is a memorial to John Ruskin on Friar's Crag. He was five years old when he first visited the place with his parents and later he recollected the visit:

> The first thing I remember as an event in life, was being taken by my nurse to the brow of Friar's Crag on Derwent Water: the intense joy mingled with awe that I had in looking through the hollows in the mossy roots, over the crag into the dark lake has ever associated itself more or less with all twining roots of trees ever since.

It is a short walk from Keswick town centre along Lake Road to the Theatre by the Lake, which hosts a programme of plays, concerts, exhibitions, readings and talks throughout the year.

The wooded peninsula of Friar's Crag, which was acquired by the National Trust in 1922.

Morning on Derwent Water.

The Boat Station, Derwent Water.

Close to it is the pier from where there are regular cruises around Derwent Water. Ferries also sail from the pier to Nichol End where almost every kind of water craft can be hired.

Leaving the pier, the ferry heads south, keeping close to the eastern side of Derwent Water. It passes between Friar's Crag and Derwent Isle and from it you can see why Friar's Crag is one of Northern Lakeland's treasures.

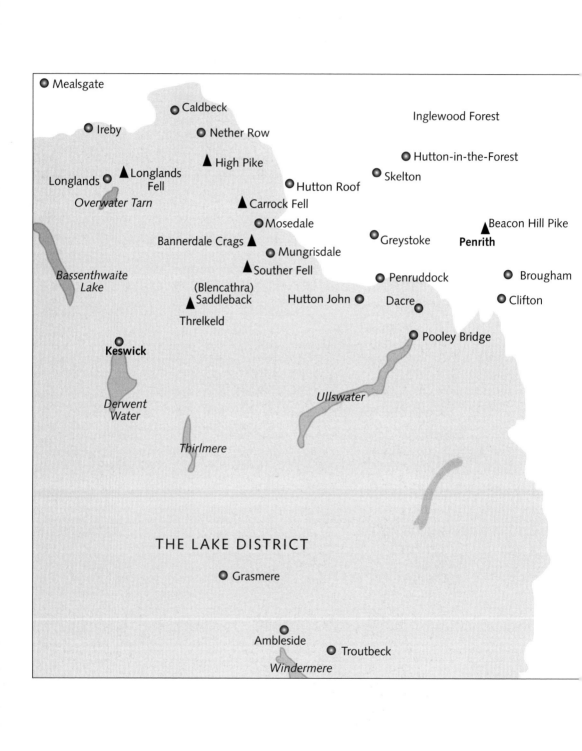

Mealsgate

Caldbeck

Ireby

Nether Row

Inglewood Forest

High Pike

Hutton-in-the-Forest

Longlands
Fell

Longlands

Skelton

Hutton Roof

Overwater Tarn

Carrock Fell

Beacon Hill Pike

Mosedale

Greystoke

Penrith

Bannerdale Crags

Mungrisdale

Bassenthwaite
Lake

Souther Fell

Penruddock

Brougham

(Blencathra)
Saddleback

Hutton John

Dacre

Clifton

Threlkeld

Keswick

Pooley Bridge

Derwent
Water

Ullswater

Thirlmere

THE LAKE DISTRICT

Grasmere

Ambleside

Troutbeck

Windermere

# 3

# The Cumbrian Mountains: North-East

## OVERWATER TARN

*OS Grid Ref: NY251350*

### 2 MILES NORTH-NORTH-EAST OF BASSENTHWAITE VILLAGE

Overwater Tarn lies on the very edge of Northern Lakeland between Binsey (1,466ft high), and Great Sca Fell (2,329ft high), the northern summit of the Skiddaw group of fells. The tarn was named after a Norseman and is the northernmost tarn in the Lake District. The northern end of the tarn has been dammed, turning it into a reservoir for Wigton. In 1992 it was handed over to the National Trust.

There is a square 'camp' south of the tarn, which is thought to have been Roman; however, it was probably the garth of an early medieval settler.

Overwater Tarn supplies Wigton with its water.

A Lakeland lady in her garden, in about 1895.

Orthwaite (Allerthwaite) Hall is less than ½ a mile south of Overwater Tarn. It has a seventeenth-century façade and over the stable door are the arms of Richmond impaling Hedleston and 'C.R. 1675'. It was the home of W.G. Brown the traveller, who was killed in Persia in 1813.

Binsey, to the west of Overwater Tarn, is set apart from the other Northern Fells; it does not even look like a fell. It is a gently rounded hill, the sort of place you would use for a gentle stroll. The summit of Binsey makes a good view point from which to study the Northern Fells; and it differs from the other fells in that its rocks are volcanic, not slate.

Great Sca Fell, to the east of Overwater Tarn, varies greatly from Binsey. In the Uldale Fells, three ridges, coming to a central point from points west to north like spokes of a wheel, meet at Great Sca Fell which is at the heart of the Uldale Fells.

Overwater Tarn has a lot going for it. If it weren't there it would be missed not only by Wigton, which it serves so well, but by countless fell walkers who find it a refreshing sight.

## LONGLANDS FELL AND VILLAGE          *OS Grid Ref: NY277354*

1¼ MILES EAST OF OVERWATER TARN

Longlands Fell is 1,580ft high and overlooks Longands village on the north-west rim of the Caldbeck Fells. The Cumbrian Way runs along the foot of Longlands Fell and through Longlands village. From Longlands village to the south-east, a long slope of fell rises steadily to the summit of a pyramid shape that is Longlands Fell. The summit is small

Very early motor cars like this one outside the inn on the top of Kirkstone Pass were used by visitors wishing to open up Northern Lakeland.

The Central Fells.

and its cairn is smaller and neater than many others. There is nothing special about the summit itself but the views from it are good. To the north-west of Longlands Fell, the land falls away beyond foothills and across flat farmland to the Solway Firth and, beyond, Scotland. Looking south, the view is somewhat restricted by higher Uldale Fells.

From Longlands village an old road goes north-eastwards to Green Head and, for anyone wishing to climb Longlands Fell from Longlands village, this is the route usually taken. Continue along this old road for just over ½ a mile. Where the old road reaches its highest point, take a bridle road that bears right, away from the old road. The bridle road you are now on begins as a peaty trod that curves to the right, gently climbing, soon to edge Charleton Gill on the left. To your right Longlands Fell rises steadily. As progress is made and the bridle road reaches a grassy groove, leave the bridle road, climbing right and aiming for the summit of Longland's Fell. The cairn makes a good 'butty' stop.

Return using the same route. The route is not demanding and is a fine introduction to the wonderful world of fell walking.

## HIGH PIKE

*OS Grid Ref: NY319351*

### 1½ MILES SOUTH OF NETHER ROW

In the nineteenth century, the vast area of fell below High Pike was exploited for a variety of minerals which, today, are no longer mined there. Much of this former industry has long gone, but enough remains in the form of adits to old mine levels to cause serious injury to an unwary fell walker. It behoves him or her to take care. Old levels penetrate deeply into the fellside and are to be avoided. Nature is a great healer and today all traces

A long view of Northern Lakeland. It is a stupendous prospect.

Cockermouth beagles ready for a hunt. Beagles resemble small foxhounds and are usually bred to hunt hares. High Pike is not really beagle territory.

of mining, apart from these adits and the odd aerial ropeway, have vanished. Where shafts have been sunk into the ground, these have been fenced off for safety's sake. Too close an inspection is not advised. Always put safety first, especially on this sort of terrain.

From Nether Row, an aerial ropeway stretched in a south-westerly direction to Potts Gill Mine to enable mined minerals to be speedily transported to an area where they could be loaded onto road transport. A route roughly alongside this disused ropeway will bring the walker to Potts Gill Mine. The way is then southwards along a track, passing several adits and keeping close to Gill Beck on the right. Soon a cluster of adits and another track are met. Continue south-westerly along the track, climbing steadily. On reaching a point where the head of a beck is reached close to an old sheep fold, leave the track and go diagonally left over undefined ground, aiming for the summit of High Pike. Here you will find a cairn and a seat. This is a good 'butty' stop with a fine north-westerly view to the Solway Firth and another south-easterly to Blencathra. These views alone will make High Pike memorable.

## CARROCK FELL
*OS Grid Ref: NY345337*

### 2 MILES WEST OF HUTTON ROOF

The Celts, warlike tribes who came from Europe in about 600 BC and settled in Northern Britain, were referred to by the Romans as Brigantes because of their allegiance to the Celtic god Brigantia. The main occupation of those who settled in Cumbria was agriculture but they were a warlike lot, who built many hill forts on the fringes of the

Bewcastle Village.

The long walk to Carrock Fell in the distance.

Lake District fells. One of the largest of these they built on the summit of Carrock Fell, 2,174ft high. The defensive stone walls of this hill fort remain. They are the largest fort remains in the north-west.

Samuel Taylor Coleridge climbed rugged Carrock Fell many times and described one especially stormy occasion in a letter dated 1800 to Humphry Davy as follows :

> on this mountain Carrock, at the summit of which are the remains of a vast circle of stones, I was wandering – when a thick cloud came on, and wrapped me in such darkness that I could not see ten yards before me – and with the cloud a storm of wind and hail, the like of which I had never before seen and felt.

Despite being advised against it by the locals, Charles Dickens and Wilkie Collins climbed Carrock Fell one wet day in 1857. Their party got lost, Dickens broke his compass and Collins fell down a ravine and sprained his ankle.

For anyone wishing to climb Carrock Fell, a good route is from near Stone Ends Farm, on the left of the unclassified road, 3½ miles south of Hesket Newmarket. From the roadside, slightly north of Stone Ends Farm, go westwards and immediately climb steeply up the eastern face of Carrock Fell, avoiding abandoned mines, which are dangerous to explore. Fallen rocks litter the steep fellside so great care is needed. However once the summit is reached, it is a great feeling. To the west the Caldbeck Fells and the Uldale Fells spread out while to the east the fells give way to fields, which stretch to the beautiful Eden Valley.

## INGLEWOOD FOREST

All the land between Carlisle and Penrith has been known for centuries as Inglewood, the forest of the Angles. However, in the beginning it was the district between the River Eden and Shawk Beck and Greystoke and Eamont. It did not include Westland, the forest to the west of Inglewood Forest. That did not become part of Inglewood Forest until it was incorporated with it under Henry II.

Following the taking of Carlisle by Ecgfrith, the Angles built their first settlements in Ingelwood Forest. Later, a Roman road was built through it as their main route from south to north. When the Normans came, Inglewood became a royal forest, which made it a royal hunting ground. Apart from a few settlements, it was largely uninhabited. Inglewood became the resort of deer stealers and outlaws until to the time of the Tudors.

Growing villages were frequently attacked by Border raiders and various earthworks and forts were used by the country-folk as refuges. Some of the earthworks date back to Norman times, while others are no older than the Elizabethan age. With such a history, Inglewood Forest is a land of romance, full of legends and curious antiquities.

By the time of William Rufus, Inglewood Forest was uncultivated and from then on the extended forest became a royal forest 'full of wood, red deer and fallow, wild swine and all manner of wild beasts.'

Working on a Northern Lakeland farm on what used to be part of Inglewood Forest.

Two or three times Inglewood Forest was granted to feudal holders but went back to the Crown and was used as part of the dower of Elizabeth I. William III granted it to Bentinck, Earl of Portland when, in the eighteenth century, it was part of the subject of a long legal struggle between the Duke of Portland and the Lowthers. In 1707 the manorial rights were sold to the Duke of Devonshire.

## SKELTON                                                    *OS Grid Ref: NY437355*

### 6 MILES NORTH-WEST OF PENRITH

The parish of Skelton has, within its bounds, Hardrigg Hall, formerly the seat of the Southaiks. It was built around a pele tower, as were many halls.

Skelton, in its early days, presented a small local show every third Saturday in August. In more recent years Skelton Village Show expanded in size, content and enterprise, incorporating aspects of an agricultural show with field events. In Cumbria, all shows are intended as much for the general visitor as for the farmer, so the distinction between the agricultural show and a sporting or field event tends to get a bit blurred. So adept have the inhabitants of Skelton become in organising their annual show that field events like Cumberland and Westmorland wrestling and hound trailing attract as many visitors as the agricultural side of things; today Skelton claims to have more animals on show than its rivals.

The means of getting to the men-folk working around Skelton village in 1903 had become outdated, but the task of providing tea to men-folk in villages throughout Cumbria never varies.

Northern Lakeland has always been primarily a livestock area, as opposed to an arable one; indeed the whole of Cumbria is renowned more for its animals than for its crops. There are more than half a million cattle, mainly for dairy, throughout Cumbria and more than one-and-a-half million sheep. All this livestock is owned by farmers who have small farms of between 50 and 100 acres. The farms around Skelton are small and owned by yeomen farmers who, with their families and perhaps a hired man, run them. They are proud folk, these Cumbrians, and like nothing better than to be left in peace to get on with their lives. They prefer, understandably, the independent sort of lifestyle places like Skelton provide to becoming swallowed up by some conglomerate, which does not have Skelton's appeal.

## HUTTON-IN-THE-FOREST                   *OS Grid Ref: NY462357*

Originally a fourteenth-century pele tower, Hutton-in-the-Forest is a wonderful piece of Arthurian legend. It is a manor in Inglewood where the Hutton family of Hutton were foresters until the time of James I, when they sold their estate to Sir Richard Fletcher. It was Richard's son, Sir Henry Fletcher, who filled in the moat and built the long gallery in about 1635. It was restored in Victorian times when the panelling was added, having probably been taken from a seventeenth-century hall. Anthony Salvin designed the library interior. When Sir Richard Fletcher's great-grandson, Sir Henry, became a monk at Douai in France, the hall went to his relatives, the Vanes, who still have it.

The church was built in 1714 on the site of an early chapel. It contains monuments of the local families and there is an interlaced pre-Norman fragment.

The great house of Hutton-in-the-Forest still hides in the remnants of a forest. The mansion's turrets and battlements contrast oddly with the part designed by Inigo Jones. Its church contains an oak lectern in memory of a man who ministered there for fifty-six years in the nineteenth century.

Inglewood, where the family of Hutton were foresters until the time of James I.

A fortified farm near Hutton-in-the-Forest.

To the north-north-west is the site of Collinwood Castle, a square rampart of about one hundred yards.

Hutton-in-the-Forest has a nice lived-in feel about it. This is because the Vanes really do live there; to the visitor it is like going to three stately homes at once. The house is open to the public on Easter Bank Holiday, then May to September, Thursday, Friday, Sunday and Bank Holidays. Parties by arrangement are welcome at any time. The gardens are open daily except Saturdays. They are very well cared for and contain some excellent tree specimens; and, yes, there is a very good tea shop. Hutton-in-the-Forest is a good day out.

## MOSEDALE AND CARROCK MINE                OS Grid Ref: NY326329

### 7½ MILES WEST-NORTH-WEST OF GREYSTOKE

A farm, some cottages and a coffee shop together become the hamlet of Mosedale. The coffee shop, which was once a Friends' Meeting House, is dated 1702, but this is not when it was built; it is when it was enlarged.

The River Caldew flows eastwards along a broad, clearly defined valley between Carrock Fell to the north and Bowscale Fell to the south, passing south of Mosedale, then curving northwards.

The Friends' Meeting House, Mosedale 1985.

Quakers suffered repression largely because of their rejection of ecclesiastical and secular hierarchies. Because of this they worshipped in secret at safe houses, like the Friends' Meeting House, Mosedale, pictured here in 1985.

A minor road goes west from Mosedale, along the Caldew Valley for 2 miles to reach Carrock Mine, which is the only one outside Devon and Cornwall to produce wolfram, the main ore-mineral of tungsten. It was a Cornishman, F.W. Emerson, who opened the mine in 1852, seeking veins of lead and copper. For half a century the mine experienced mixed fortunes under several owners. In 1906, a new Cumbrian Mining Company, financed by two Germans, boosted excavations. Over 100 workers were employed there. However, within five years the Cumbrian Mining Company went out of business. In 1913 a Carrock Mining Syndicate, backed with government finance, bought the mine, introduced new equipment and electricity. After the First World War the mine fell into disuse and it was not used again until 1942 when Canadian Royal Engineers worked it. When they were moved on, Italian prisoners of war and Spaniards worked the mine. There followed a period when the mine suffered more mixed fortunes. It finally closed in 1981.

## MUNGRISDALE COMMON             *Summit OS Grid Ref: NY312292*

### 8 MILES WEST-SOUTH-WEST OF GREYSTOKE

Mungrisdale Common covers a large part of the eastern buttress of the Skiddaw group of fells. The southern part of this vast, featureless pancake of uninteresting land rises to become the bland north-west aspect of Saddleback.

The lack of distinguishing features on Mungrisdale Common highlights the grandeur of Blencathra (Saddleback), the northern side of which is part of Mungrisdale Common.

To the south-west of Mungrisdale Common, Roughton Gill and Sinen Gill drain into Glenderaterra Beck. There are two waterfalls close together on Roughton Gill and Sinen Gill also has one.

A fence runs from south to north along the bottom of a depression that separates Mungrisdale Common from Lonscale Fell. Midway along this fence, a stake, which is a boundary stone, is set alongside it. Anyone walking northwards alongside this fence on the left, should turn right at the stake and climb the grassy slope. Soon a rock called the Cloven Stone is reached. Continue past it, climbing less steeply, for about a mile to reach the summit of Mungrisdale Common.

Because no cairn or any other distinguishing features mark the summit, the exact spot is not clear; one clump of cotton grass looks very much like another. However there is no doubt about the height of the summit; it is 2,068ft above sea level.

Two other 'sikes' (very thin becks), White Gill and Blackhazel Beck, flow northwards into the River Caldew, which takes a north-easterly course before curving east along the Mosedale Valley.

Hikers are as rare as hen's teeth on Mungrisdale Common, which large as it is, accommodates only sheep, mostly hardy Herdwicks, and their shepherds. This is a part of Northern Lakeland that has no appeal to strangers and little appeal to the locals. It is uninviting, to be sure, but those who have seen this weary landscape tend to appreciate more fully the magnificent scenery the rest of Northern Lakeland has to offer.

## BANNERDALE CRAGS                    *Summit OS Grid Ref: NY336291*

### 2 MILES SOUTH-WEST OF MUNGRISDALE VILLAGE

Bannerdale Crags mark the eastern end of Mungrisdale Common. They form a mile-long gentle curve and reach their highest point at 2,230ft, about a third of the way along them from their southern end. Beneath the highest point a spur, the East Ridge, cuts through the escarpment. Elsewhere the escarpment falls steeply into the small side-valley of Bannerdale, which was once a swamp. At the western end of Bannerdale, at the foot of Bannerdale Crags, there used to be a lead mine, which has been closed for many years.

Mungrisdale village is a good starting point for anyone wishing to climb Bannerdale Crags. Leave the village along a wide path to the north of the River Glenderamackin. Where the river's course makes a south-west turn, keep straight ahead, aiming for the foot of the steep slope on the left side of The Tongue. Continue along the left-hand side of the tongue for a mile, following a path that climbs steadily. During the ascent, where the path bifurcates, take the clearer, right-hand one, still climbing. Soon a pair of upright stones can be seen ahead. They mark the top of the scarp. On reaching them, turn left, along the top of Bannerdale Crags until you have reached their highest point. Just past the summit cairns, turn left, and make a very steep descent of the East Ridge into narrow, steep-sided Bannerdale. As the valley bottom is reached, keep straight ahead to reach the River Glenderamackin where Bannerdale Beck joins it. Here, turn left, cross the

Hardy Swaledale sheep which, together with Herdwicks, a native Cumberland breed, are at home on the fells.

beck and continue edging the River Glenderamackin, which is only a beck, until the track you are on meets the one used on the outward leg. Continue along it, retracing your steps back to Mungrisdale village, having explored Bannerdale Crags, which many visitors to Northern Lakeland have never seen.

## MUNGRISDALE VILLAGE                    *OS Grid Ref: NY364303*

4 MILES NORTH-WEST OF PENRUDDOCK
Mungrisdale was formerly called Mungo-Grisedale, Swinedale of St Mungo's church. Mungo is the name by which St Kentigern was known to those close to him and the village church is dedicated to him. St Kentigern's church was established in Mungrisdale village in AD 552 but by the time the spectral army of nearby Souther Fell had been seen by a group of respected locals (see page 113), Mungrisdale no longer had a church. A replacement church, the present one, dates from 1756.

A memorial on the church wall commemorates Raisley Calvert, who had a son also called Raisley. The younger Raisley was a sculptor who became a good friend of William

Mungrisdale church is dedicated to St Kentigern.

Mungrisdale village, to the east of Bannerdale Crags, edges good cattle pasture like this.

Mungrisdale village, which celebrates its annual Pie Festival every October.

Wordsworth. When the younger Raisley became ill with consumption (tuberculosis), Wordsworth spent many hours by his bedside in Penrith Hospital. Sadly, the younger Raisley died in 1795. He left the large amount of £900 to his loyal friend in his will. The bequest could not have come at a more fortuitous time for Wordsworth, for it enabled the poet to complete a project on which he was working with his friend Coleridge. This was the production of important poems published in 1798 as the *Lyrical Ballads*.

The Mill Inn is Mungrisdale village's 'local' and, appropriately, a stone mill wheel props up the bar. The food served in both the restaurant and the bar is reasonably priced and good, with home made pies a speciality. Every October, the pub celebrates its annual Pie Festival.

The Mill Hotel is situated very close to the Mill Inn, but the two are different entities. The hotel provides an intimate, highly personalised country house experience. So, between the two, you have a good choice and both are well worth visiting.

## SOUTHER FELL AND THE PHANTOM ARMY          *OS Grid Ref: NY356292*

It is neither the height of Souther Fell (1,680ft), nor the fact that it is pronounced 'Souter' that makes it notorious. No, what gives it notoriety is something far stranger than that. On midsummer's eve 1735, a farm servant saw that the eastern side of the summit ridge of Souther Fell was covered with troops which, for an hour, marched to disappear into a niche in the summit. When he told the villagers of nearby Mungrisdale what he had seen he was ridiculed.

Two years later, the whole family of the farm where he worked saw the same thing; they too, were thought to have gone mad.

On midsummer's eve 1745, twenty-six local folk all saw an army, 'a multitude beyond imagining,' only this time with horse-drawn carriages. Yet how the carriages could have been on Souther Fell is puzzling because the fell's sides are too steep for horse-drawn carriages to climb.

Each of those twenty-six people attested what they had seen on oath before a magistrate and the following day they climbed to the ridge summit of Souther Fell looking for footprints and wheel marks. They found nothing, which was very odd because they had seen an army on the march up there. So many soldiers with horse-drawn carriages could not have crossed Souther Fell without leaving any indentations on the ground. Yet there it was; no marks of any kind.

It transpired that a Jacobite army had been marching that evening, but a long way away to the north. It was supposed that the ghostly figures seen on Souther Fell were a reflection of these Jacobites. It was an unlikely explanation, discounted by many.

Other small groups of ghostly figures have been seen on Souther Fell from time to time. Always they have been on the eastern side of the summit ridge and always travelling from north to south.

Souther Fell and Saddleback.

It is always along the eastern ridge of Souther Fell that the phantom army marches, moving north to south (right to left) in the picture. Saddleback is seen in the background.

Good farmland seen from Souther Fell, looking eastwards.

Souther Fell in peaceful mood.

# SADDLEBACK OR BLENCATHRA

*OS Grid Ref: NY323278*

## 5 MILES NORTH-EAST OF KESWICK

Saddleback was originally called Blencathra. The name 'Blencathra' is Celtic and 'Saddleback' describes the shape of the mountain, as seen from the south-east. It is made of the same slate as Skiddaw, but with fierce-looking steep cliffs on its south side caused by moving glaciers, it looks a larger mountain than it actually is.

Wainwright called it a mountaineer's mountain and it is one of the finest landmarks in the Lake District. Its summit is 2,847ft high.

Saddleback compels attention. Its southern aspect is dramatic, a 3¼-mile-long series of five buttresses, the outer two being covered with grass, the inner three with heather. All the inner three rise to peaks, the central one being Saddleback's summit. Each buttress is named after a fell which, from west to east, are Gategill Fell, Hall's Fell and Doddick Fell.

Scales Tarn lies under crags to the north of Doddick Fell. In 'The Bridal of Triermain', Sir Walter Scott alludes to the story that this tarn lies in such a hollow that it reflects the stars at noon. The water in Scales Tarn is always too cold for fish to live in it.

Sharp Edge, originally called Razor Edge, soars above the north side of Scales Tarn. It is the narrowest edge in the Lake District. It climbs in a most spectacular and dangerous way to Foule Crag, an equally nasty rock formation just below Blencathra's saddle. There is one particularly awkward place on Sharp Edge, where experienced fell-walkers

Looking towards Keswick from Threlkeld, which is sited at the southern foot of Blencathra or Saddleback, seen rising steeply on the right.

Souther Fell fronting magnificent Blencathra or Saddleback.

must traverse sloping rock then make an ungainly shuffle onto more sloping rocks. Inexperienced walkers should not attempt this route. Crossing Sharp Edge should not be attempted in wet and windy weather and great care must be taken at all times.

Do not be afraid to try an alternative route. There are at least a dozen ways to reach the summit of Saddleback. The best and most direct way is from Threlkeld, climbing Hall's Fell Top where a cairn marks the summit of Saddleback. A. Wainwright called this route the finest way to any mountain top in the district; he was so right.

## MEALSGATE

*OS Grid Ref: NY209420*

### 4 MILES EAST OF ASPATRIA

Mealsgate is a working Cumbrian village sited in good farming country at the foot of the northern fells. It has no pretensions about being a visitor honey-pot. Farming has been its preoccupation for centuries and that is how the locals like it.

For many years, while the means of getting in the hay may have changed, dependence on fine weather still plays an important part. The local blacksmith has to adapt to new methods of working, but demands on his time are as strong as they ever were, just like the beer in the local.

Mealsgate blacksmith and family, 1910.

Making hay while the sun shines.

For many long months the grass in the meadows has been getting taller. Once midsummer's day has passed, the farmers begin casting anxious eyes at the weather; a spell of wet could ruin the whole hay harvest.

The state of the weather played an important part in the decision to begin cutting the hay. Once the farmer had decided it was all systems go, as many extra hands as possible were hired for the period of the haymaking. Many of these were itinerant Irish workers and although many were sound dependable folk, some were not so reliable.

At one place, the farmer hired several men for hay time, but before they could start, the weather changed and it began to rain. The inclement weather persisted for all the weeks the Irishmen had been hired, and they stayed at the farm, were fed and paid and did absolutely nothing. By the end of what would have been the length of the hay time agreement, the weather cleared up. The farmer asked them if they would stay with him until the hay was gathered in. They refused.

## GREYSTOKE CASTLE, HOME OF TARZAN, LORD OF THE APES

*OS Grid Ref: NY435307*

### 5½ MILES WEST OF PENRITH

Greystoke Castle is the seat of an ancient barony which included all Cumberland between Inglewood, Penrith and Castlerigg (Keswick). Lyulf is said to have received it from Ranulf de Mechines before 1120. In 1506, heiress Elizabeth of Greystone married Thomas Lord

Greystoke village. Two surrounding farmhouses have American associations: Bunkers Hill and Fort Putnam. Greystoke Castle was burned down twice. It has been owned by the Greystokes, the Dacres and, currently, the Howards.

Dacre of Gilsland and from then the Dacres were Lords of Greystoke until 1569 when their heiress married Philip Howard, Earl of Arundel. From then on, Greystoke Castle has been the seat of the Howards of Greystoke.

In 1984, Greystoke Castle was perpetuated as the ancestral home of Tarzan, Lord of the Apes in the film *Greystoke*, based on the famous character created by Edgar Rice Burroughs in 1912. Burroughs, an American born in Chicago, never visited England.

The effigies of all the Barons of Greystoke (except Tarzan) are preserved in Greystoke church, which is dedicated to St Andrew. The church is an impressive structure, as spacious as a cathedral. Its east window contains much thirteenth-century glass and its bells are ancient. In the Lady Chapel there is a figure of the Madonna and Child which was carved by a German prisoner of war.

About 100 yards from the church there is a plague stone. It marks where, during medieval times, people suffering from the plague would place coins into vinegar to pay for food. A soaking in vinegar prevented the spread of the plague.

When Shelley and his wife stayed at Greystoke for the first week of December 1811, he constantly complained about the aristocratic stupidity he found there; but he was in no hurry to leave.

The famous Gordon W. Richards racing stable has its home at Greystoke. Hundreds of winners have been trained there, including two winners of the Grand National.

Greystoke Castle.

# IREBY

## 1 MILE NORTH-WEST OF HESKET NEWMARKET

Ireby, on the northern edge of the Lakes, gained a market charter in the thirteenth century, but in time Wigton and Cockermouth proved too much competition for it. It shrank from being a little market town to being a village. Its market cross spent a long time in ruins, but has now been restored.

More pathetic than the decay of the town is the decay of a small building in the fields 1½ miles away. It is a simple Norman church to which the people of Ireby walked to worship. They did so for many centuries. Sadly, this lonely building was left to die a lingering death among the graves of those who used to worship in it.

Ireby now has a new church in the village. In it are an ancient font with four carved roundels and two old stones built into the walls of the church. These have all been rescued from the original church. One of these stones has shears and some crosses carved on it. The other has an ornate cross and a sword. They are the memorial of John de Ireby who lived over 700 years ago.

This peaceful region is well off the tourist track and offers visitors a delightful landscape of gently undulating fells and valleys sheltering unspoilt villages like Ireby.

Ireby is a good base from which to explore the Solway Coast, Bassenthwaite and Skiddaw.

Like most Cumbrian villages, Ireby had its own dancing master, who supervised a dancing school at the Sun Inn. One day, Keats and his friend Charles Brown called at the Sun Inn and were greatly amused to watch members of the dancing school performing a new cotillion, an eighteenth-century French formation dance. Even in those days, Cumbrian villages knew what was happening in other countries.

A farmer and his dog working with cattle.

Ireby Mill and Ireby village, 1900.

## THRELKELD

*OS Grid Ref: NY320255*

### 3 MILES NORTH-EAST OF KESWICK

Threlkeld is a scattered village tucked under the southern slope of Saddleback. A settlement has been there since Neolithic times and it has thrived for centuries on its granite quarries and mines. Above the quarries there are some ancient stone circles; and some cairns are close to an old packhorse track that leads to Wanthwaite.

Threlkeld's church, St Mary's, was rebuilt in 1814 and has two medieval bells.

Threlkeld Hall, the seat of James Threlkeld, became ruinous many years ago and has now become part of a farmhouse. In the fifteenth century, an earlier Threlkeld, Sir Launcelot, used to boast that he had three noble houses: one for pleasure at Crosby in Westmorland, with a park full of deer; one for profit and warmth at Yanwath, 'nigh Penrith' and one at Threlkeld, well stocked with tenants to go with him to the wars.

Sir Launcelot married into the Clifford family. During the Battle of Towton, when Lord Clifford was killed, Sir Launcelot took Lord Clifford's son into his care, working on the Threlkeld estate as a shepherd.

Sir Launcelot is buried in the church at Crosby Ravensworth.

Today Threlkeld is famous for its annual sheep dog trials.

Threlkeld Mining Museum has a superb collection of small mining and quarrying artefacts including wedges, chisels, drills, candles, clogs and kibbles which are large iron buckets used to transport ore.

Visitors are also allowed to browse through Threlkeld Quarry and Mining Museum, with its collection of vintage excavators, old quarry machinery and other artefacts.

Portinscale Bridge, fronting Lakeland fell country.

Threlkeld is found on the southern edge of Skiddaw Forest, sitting in the shadow of Saddleback. It is the home of the Blencathra foxhounds, and the local inn, the Horse and Farrier serves a good pint.

## TROUTBECK                                      *OS Grid Ref: NY389272*

### 5 MILES NORTH-EAST OF WINDERMERE

Designated a conservation area, Troutbeck village has no recognisable centre. Its houses and cottages are grouped around a number of wells and springs which until recently were the only source of water.

Troutbeck church has a fine east window by Burne-Jones that dates from 1873. One of its vicars was the remarkable the Revd Mr Sewell who, one day in the early nineteenth century, was crossing Kirkstone Pass from Patterdale when he found a pack woman half frozen to death, and carried her down to Troutbeck. He caused an inn to be built at the top of that lofty pass for others who might find themselves in the same predicament. The Revd Mr Sewell is buried in Troutbeck churchyard.

Many of the buildings in Troutbeck are built in the Lake District vernacular style. The most interesting is, perhaps, Townend Farm, a National Trust property. The Browne family, very wealthy farmers, lived there for 300 years until 1944. They were responsible for the fine carved woodwork inside the building as well as furniture, books and domestic implements collected down the years. In the 1890s, George, the last of the Brownes, added to the impressive display of oak furniture in Townend Farm by improving the earlier pieces with extra carvings. Much of what visitors now see bears the hallmark of the last of the Brownes.

Troutbeck is backed by high fells, just like Rosthwaite, pictured here in about 1900.

An old cottage in Troutbeck, on the left.

Thomas Hogarth, who lived in Troutbeck, became known as the 'Troutbeck Giant'. He was the uncle of the painter William Hogarth.

There are two pubs at Troutbeck; both are old. One is Queens, the other is Mortal Man. The latter takes its odd name from its sign painted by Julius Caesar Ibbotson, in about 1800. It shows a lean and a fat man, 'portraits of natives' and the following rhyme:

> Thou mortal man lives by bread,
> How comes thy nose to be so red?
> Thou silly ass, that looks so pale,
> It is by drinking Sarah Birkett's ale.

## HUTTON JOHN

*OS Grid Ref: NY439268*

### 1 MILE WEST OF DACRE

Hutton John is one of Cumberland's old-fashioned manor houses. Its 600-year-old pele tower has had both a Tudor wing and a Stuart wing added. It was held from the fourteenth century by the Huttons, passing, during the reign of Queen Elizabeth I, by marriage to the Huddlestons, one of whom, John, was a Roman Catholic priest who followed Charles II after the Battle of Worcester and became the king's private confessor.

Two's company: three's a crowd. This photograph, taken near Ullswater, was awarded the photographic Gold Medal in 1898.

Cars – not one to be seen! Here, pedestrians are walking through a Cumbrian village without fear of being knocked over by a car. Yes, there used to be such days.

The gardens are a delight. There are two Tudor terraces with eight magnificent yews. For generations they grew in a great hedge and they have been clipped to their present shape for well over a century. A natural curiosity is a limestone rockery formed by the hard water of a hillside spring. Inside a little grotto, the water is turning the moss into stone because of the heavy concentration of lime in it.

In 1802 William and Dorothy Wordsworth explored the countryside near Hutton John. They found that the land needed to be drained, the hedges were neglected and that bracken was spreading everywhere. Trees were scattered across the steep sides of the hills that sloped to the stony bedrock of the River Eamont, making them look like parkland.

Today the whole area is very well husbanded. Even Dacre Castle, at the head of the valley, has been restored to its former glory.

# DACRE                                  *OS Grid Ref: NY458265*

### 4 MILES WEST-SOUTH-WEST OF PENRITH

Dacre, a quiet village in the valley of the Eamont, was originally called Dacor. It is guarded by a castle that defended it from Border raiders. It is thought that Aethelstan of England, grandson of Alfred the Great, and Constantine, King of Scotland, signed a peace treaty in AD 926. It was called the Peace of Dacre. Aethelstan was a powerful warrior king to whom the pagan kings swore allegiance and were baptised into Christianity.

Dacre church occupies the site of a former monastery, which was mentioned by the Venerable Bede in his accounts of Cumberland in the eighth century. The church was built in the nineteenth century, rather oddly on the side of a great pyramid hill. It has an Elizabethan altar cup; and there is a piece of medieval gravestone in the churchyard. Canon Wilson, who preached there for forty years, did many of the carvings in the church. The chancel was panelled and ornamented by him. He fashioned the little angels on the pulpit and he created much of the church furniture. Canon Wilson was buried in the churchyard in 1921.

Skybarrow Crag, Ullswater, the closest lake to Dacre.

Dacre Castle, the seat of the Dacres.

The castle seems huge for so small a village. It has a massive keep, complete with turrets and battlements, and walls that are 7ft thick. It began as a fourteenth-century pele tower, a defence against raiding Scots.

There are four weather-beaten carvings of bears in the churchyard. They are probably Anglo-Viking and are shown respectively being attacked by a cat, shaking it off, eating it and sleeping.

Castle, church and village are all highly picturesque.

## POOLEY BRIDGE                                                    *OS Grid Ref: NY470245*

The pleasant village of Pooley Bridge is sited at the northern lip of Ullswater, the lake that in Wordsworth's opinion, provided 'the happiest combination of beauty and grandeur, which any of the lakes affords.'

Regular cruises depart from Pooley Bridge during the summer season and the best way to see Ullswater is from one of these cruises.

Originally, Pooley Bridge was known as Pooley, which was derived from 'a pool by the hill'. The hill is called Dunmallard and the remains of an Iron Age fort are on its summit. Pooley developed along both sides of the Eamont, the river that hereabouts marked the boundary between Cumberland and Westmorland. When a bridge was built

Pooley Bridge is on the River Eamont at the foot of Ullswater. Nearby Dunmallard is perhaps the site of a fort, but is neither Roman nor a monastery. South-west of Pooley Bridge there used to be earthworks, thought to have been a lake dwelling.

Ullswater from Place Fell, a favourite walk of Wainwright.

across the Eamont at Pooley, the village's name became Pooley Bridge. It used to be a very busy place with a regular market including a fish market and a sheep and cattle fair. Unfortunately, Pooley Bridge's markets were regularly overshadowed by those at nearby Penrith and never really developed. There are two main streets in Pooley Bridge, both of which are lined with charming stone houses. The oldest building in Pooley Bridge is part of Holly House, which dates back to 1691. The elegant bridge over the River Eamont, which cost £400 to build, was constructed in 1763. The views down Ullswater from Pooley Bridge are a wonderful asset for the village which caters mainly for tourists.

From Pooley Bridge it is an easy walk of a couple of miles, south-east, to Moor Divock, crossing a Roman Road en route. Moor Divock is set among many interesting pre-historic cairns, which have contained interments. Some had burnt bones in urns; one had a skeleton in a stone coffin made of slabs. There are lots of such remains. Anyone addicted to cairns need look no further than Askham Fell.

Red deer are at home in these surroundings. They are free to roam all over the Martindale Fells and bring a touch of colour to the scene.

## CLIFTON                                                      *OS Grid Ref: NY533268*

### 2 MILES SOUTH OF PENRITH

Clifton is a village near Lowther, the seat of the Earl of Lowther, the 'yellow Earl'. It was at Clifton Moor, south of Clifton, that the last skirmish was ever fought by armies on English soil. It took place in December 1745, when Bonnie Prince Charlie was in retreat. The Scots were easily routed by the English army and eleven soldiers were killed and were buried where they fell. Some of the wounded highlanders were hanged from the Jacobite Rebel Tree on the outskirts of Clifton.

Stockdale Wath village which, like Clifton, depends greatly on farming.

Old Toll-Bar, near Keswick.

Two monuments are reminders of this skirmish. A small one stands inside Clifton churchyard to the right of the entrance. It commemorates those of Cumberland's dragoons who died in the action.

Wetherigg's County Pottery is at the south-east of Clifton. It was founded in 1855. This pottery is steam-powered, the only one of its kind in Britain. The pottery was scheduled as an Industrial Monument in 1973 and its steam engine was restored by Fred Dibnah, the famous steeplejack. Visitors can try their hand at the messy business of 'throwing' a pot, painting a pot, painting glass, or making a candle. The pottery has a tearoom, several shops and a pond that is home to some newts.

## BROUGHAM CASTLE AND ARTHUR'S ROUND TABLE

*OS Grid Ref: NY538289*

### ½ A MILE SOUTH-EAST OF PENRITH

Originally called Burgham, Brougham Castle, pronounced 'Broom', stands at the site of a Roman camp thought to have been Brocavum. The ruins of the castle, north of the camp and close to the River Eamont, are in an irregular moated boundary wall and form a small court with a Norman Keep to which was added a gatehouse on the north with a doorway inscribed 'Thys made Roger' (de Clifford, late thirteenth century), who also

The Toll House at Brougham, near Penrith.

Brougham Castle plays a prominent part in a 'Greetings from Lakeland' postcard.

raised the keep higher and built the hall on the south-east side. James I is said to have spent three days there in 1617. The moat was restored by Lady Anne Clifford, Countess of Pembroke in the seventeenth century.

Arthur's Round Table at Eamont Bridge, 1 mile upstream of Brougham Castle on the River Eamont, is a platform 73ft by 72ft, enclosed by an oval trench. The trench is surrounded by an embankment 7ft high at its highest part. To the south-east, a gangway leads to the platform. There used to be another gangway opposite, but this has been cut off by a road. The origin of Arthur's Round Table is not known, but it was once used for games. A plan by Pennant, dated 1769, shows a second ring embankment to the south, called the Little Round Table.

A great circular stone rampart south-west of Eamont Bridge is 383ft in diameter from crest to crest, with an opening to the east and a standing stone 9ft 2in high near its centre. The ruins of a wall on the crest are modern. A bronze celt (an implement with a chisel-edge) and a stone celt have been found there; but there is no sign of any burial.

## PENRITH

### 5 MILES EAST-NORTH-EAST OF KESWICK

Penrith, pronounced Peerith, is in a red sandstone area and was certainly a place of importance from very early, though not Roman, times. In Saxon times it was the capital of the Kingdom of Cumbria. Ancient crosses and hogbacks in the parish churchyard were re-arranged a long time ago to form what is known as the 'Giant's Grave', and the isolated crosses called the 'Giant's Thumb' must be 1,000 years old and their size and number indicate that important people were buried there. The church was rebuilt between 1720 and 1722 and contains many interesting monuments.

Penrith was especially open to Scottish raids, both because it was on the road from the north and because it was one of the places claimed by the Scottish Kings in the grant that gave John Balliol certain manors in compensation for abandoning the whole of the northern counties of England. When Edward I resumed these manors, the Scots thought it was their duty to make them worthless so in 1347 Douglas wasted Penrith and in 1382 it was burned. From about 1397 the Nevilles held Penrith for fifty years and built the castle. Later it was the residence of Richard III, then Duke of Gloucester.

Protected by the castle, Penrith flourished. It had received a market charter in 1223 and in 1340 got its first school. In about 1400 a water supply was brought to Penrith from Petterill by Bishop Strickland. A little known priory of Austin Friars was on the site of the friarage. After 1543 the castle was disused. Penrith as a manor formed part of the dowry of successive queens and border raids did not reach so far. In the seventeenth century the town became what it still is, the great market for the neighbourhood. The moot hall, cross, stocks and shambles were removed 200 years ago but several buildings of antiquity remain.

Penrith, 1904. There has been a settlement here since before the Romans arrived. They appreciated its position on the main west-coast artery between England and Scotland and built a fort close to it. Today Penrith is the most historic of all the towns in Lakeland.

Penrith corn market in about 1900. Penrith is a charming mix of wide open spaces into which cattle were herded during raids by Scots, and narrow streets. Later, the wide spaces became market places and Penrith still holds a market every Tuesday.

Penrith corn market from the west, in the early twentieth century.

# BEACON HILL PIKE

*OS Grid Ref: NY522314*

Beacon Hill Pike is a tower that dominates Penrith. It stands in the middle of a wooded slope on the north side of the town. The tower was built in 1719 on the spot where, from 1296, beacons were lit to warn the householders of impending Scottish attacks.

The beacon was last lit in 1804, during the Napoleonic Wars; one of those who saw it was Sir Walter Scott, who was visiting Cumberland at the time. Seeing it prompted him to hurry home and rejoin his local volunteer regiment.

On one occasion, while still a boy, William Wordsworth lost his guide in mist on Beacon Hill and became scared. Leading his horse, he stumbled downhill and reached the spot where Thomas Nicholson, a murderer, had been hanged in chains from a gibbet in 1767. The gibbet had crumbled away, the skeleton and the iron case were gone, but the murderer's name had been carved into the nearby tree. This petrified William Wordsworth and haunted him throughout his life.

Nicholson's ghost, hanging from a noose, is rumoured to still be there.

Cutting timber on Beacon Hill, 1907.

As teenagers, Dorothy Wordsworth and Mary Hutchinson frequently walked on Beacon Hill. Sometimes, William Wordsworth would go with them during his summer holidays. It is quite likely that he formed an attachment to Mary Hutchinson, whom he later married, on Beacon Hill.

Many of Penrith's Victorian houses were built of the red sandstone quarried along the escarpments of Beacon Edge. One of the quarries is now a nature reserve, and a Site of Special Scientific Interest. The rocks are the remains of sand dunes formed 250 million years ago.

# 4

# Cumbrian Customs, Characters and Pastimes

## ANCIENT SETTLERS AND MODERN 'BOON'

Although the Danes and Saxons invaded much of England, they only reached some of the fertile plains on the western slopes of Lakeland. It was the Norse who colonised Cumbria during the ninth and tenth centuries. Unlike the Danes, who were brutal, the Vikings did not invade in warlike droves. They gradually filtered into Lakeland, coming down the west coast of Scotland to Ireland and the Isle of Man. They entered Lakeland from the west and established themselves, farming the land extensively. They have left an indelible mark in local words. 'Dales' comes from *'dair'*, 'fell' from *'fjall'*, 'beck' from *'beick'* and

'Boon' ploughing at Hesket Hall, 1908.

Haytime. Here the grass is being cut, strewn to dry, then cocked before being led away for winter storage.

Sheep-shearing day at Wood Hall Farm, in about 1960.

A boon sheep clipping day at Wood Hall, a Cumberland farm, in about 1960. The method employed is exactly the same as at Bitts Park, Carlisle.

'tarn' from *'tjorn'*. 'Force', meaning waterfall, comes from *'foss'* and many Cumbrian place-names end in 'thwaite', which is from the Norse for 'clearing in forest'.

It has long been a Cumbrian custom for locals to help people who have come from 'outside' and bought a farm there or are locals in the process of buying their first farm. Neighbours all gather around and help the newcomers become established as smoothly as possible. This means of helping newcomers feel at home is called doing a 'boon' and takes different forms according to the time of year in which it takes place. It could involve help with sheep-shearing or assisting with getting the hay in at hay time or ploughing. This help is very much appreciated by the recipient of the assistance who, in turn, will do his share to help people in a similar situation in the future. 'Boon' is an admirable facet of Lakeland life because it helps to bond together Lakeland life.

## THE TRAVELLING DENTIST

A small but very important part of the Cumbrian scene has been the travelling dentist, who would visit outlying schools on a regular basis to inspect the teeth of the pupils and take what action was needed. This usually meant fillings or extractions, and ensured that pupils with dental problems had them dealt with at an early stage. It was a good practice that worked well but on occasion, unexpected problems did happen. One such example

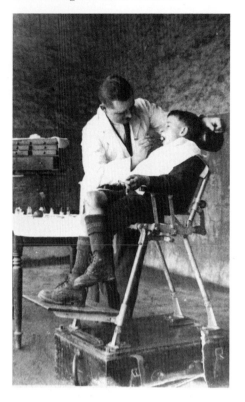

'Open wide and don't burn your finger!'

is of the travelling dentist making one of his regular visits to Kirkby Stephen and his hand drill snapped in two inside a pupil's mouth. The dentist told the pupil not to close his mouth, then moved away. The pupil could not close his mouth anyway because, when he tried to do so, the sharp broken end of the drill stuck into the roof of his mouth. The pupil had no other option but to keep his mouth firmly open until the dentist returned and removed the offending piece of broken drill. It seemed an age, but, in reality, it was only a few seconds. However, it was long enough for the pupil, myself in fact, to form an uncomplimentary opinion of dentists.

Many years before this incident, a local dentist died. He was buried in the churchyard at the village of Outhgill, in Mallerstang. On his headstone below his name, were the words

DENTIST.

FILLING HIS LAST CAVITY.

During the years leading up to the Second World War, smoking was 'de rigueur' and most people indulged in it.

Sometimes dentists would smoke a cigarette while at work. The one pictured above, seeing that he could not pull out a tooth while smoking, gets his boy patient to take hold of his cigarette for him. It was a satisfactory arrangement.

## THE LAKE POETS

The term, 'Lake Poets', is more a piece of literary terminology than an indicator of a true clique of like-minded individuals. In fact the 'Lake Poets' had little in common except an interest in the landscape.

Robert Southey was born at Bristol in 1774 and educated at Westminster and Oxford. In 1795 he married Edith Fricker, whose sister was already married to Samuel Taylor Coleridge. Several years later, the Southeys went to live at Greta Hall, Keswick, which they shared with the Coleridges. The Coleridges soon left for Malta but Robert Southey remained in Keswick for the rest of his life. From 1808 he became the greatest Tory journalist of his day and in 1813 he was made Poet Laureate. He died in 1843 and was buried in Crosthwaite churchyard alongside his wife and children.

Robert Southey, poet laureate and Lake Poet.

Inside Grasmere Church, where William Wordsworth worshipped.

Samuel Taylor Coleridge (1772–1834), son of a clergyman, was born in Devonshire and educated at Christ's Hospital and Cambridge where he became an enthusiastic supporter of the French Revolution. In 1799 he fell in love with the sister of Wordsworth's future wife. However, he was devoted to the children of his own marriage and recognised the impossibility of dissolving it. In 1800 the Coleridges moved to Keswick to be near Wordsworth. When the Southeys later joined them there was friction at home and Coleridge left his family to Southey's care. Coleridge was a great walker and the pioneer of rock climbing. In August 1802 he made a nine-day walking tour taking in the peaks and valleys of the central and western lakes in a 100-mile circuit, his way of escaping his troubled marriage. He was an insatiable reader, master of brilliant conversation and had great charm. Coleridge made a remarkable contribution to English literature. On hearing of his death, Wordsworth called him 'the most wonderful man he had ever known.'

William Wordsworth (1770–1850), was born at Cockermouth and had an undistinguished career at Cambridge followed by a year in France at the height of the revolution where he met Annette Vallon who bore him a daughter. Returning to England, he came into a legacy which enabled he and his sister, Dorothy, to live near Coleridge in Somerset. In 1799 William and Dorothy settled in Grasmere. William married Mary Hutchinson, a childhood friend, in 1802. In 1843 he became Poet Laureate.

## JOHN RUSKIN: THE LONDON CONNECTION

John Ruskin, the art critic, writer, social reformer and artist was born in London in 1819. He first came to the Lakes in 1824. When he was eleven years old he visited St Mary's Church, Carlisle Cathedral, and wrote in his diary:

> We were lucky in procuring a seat near that of Mr Wordsworth, there being only one between it and the one we were in. We were rather disappointed in this gentleman's appearance, especially as he appeared asleep the greater part of the time! He seemed about sixty. This gentleman possesses a long face and a large nose with a moderate assortment of grey hairs and two small eyes, grey but filled with fury wrapt, inspired with a mouth of moderate dimensions that is quite large enough to let in sufficient quantity of beef or mutton and to let out a sufficient quantity of poetry.

The John Ruskin memorial, Friar's Crag, Keswick.

Brantwood, Ruskin's home at
Coniston Water.

John Ruskin, famed art critic, outside
his Brantwood home where he died
in 1900.

In 1867, Ruskin called Blencathra:

> the finest thing I have yet seen, (in Cumberland), there being several bits of real crag work and a fine view at the top over the great plain of Penrith on one side and the Cumberland hills as a chain on the other. Fine, fresh wind blowing and plenty of crows… there were some of the biggest and hoarsest-voiced ones about the cliff that I have ever had sympathetic croaks from.

As a precocious twelve-year-old, John Ruskin described an early Victorian climb of Skiddaw:

> At length here stand we, wrapt in cloud
> In which light dwelt before the sun was born,
> Alone and in a shroud
> Of dazzling mist, while the wind, whistling loud
> Buffets thy streaming looks – result forlorn
> For us.

He maintained that mountains were the beginning and the end of all natural scenery and described Friar's Crag as 'one of the three most beautiful scenes in Europe.'

John Ruskin spent the last twenty-nine years of his life at Brantwood on the east shore of Coniston Water, where locals lived in awe of him. He died there in 1900. A monument of local stone marks his grave.

## HERDWICKS

The Herdwick is a native Cumbrian breed of sheep, usually found grazing the Lakeland uplands like the wilderness of Mungrisdale Common. Herdwicks are peculiar to high fell country, living in conditions which other breeds of sheep would struggle to survive in. The hill farmers who breed them usually have fields surrounding their farms and their Herdwicks are often put into these fields, where the pickings are slightly better than on the fells. Sometimes the Herdwicks are sold to farmers living in the valley bottoms where conditions are much better for them.

Herwicks are better suited to the harsh conditions of Lakeland than most other breeds of sheep, but they are not the most popular. There are several reasons for this. They tend not to grow very fat, their wool is coarse and they are not prolific breeders. The Swaledale, which is also a hardy creature, has a far better reproductive record than the Herdwick. However, the conditions in which Herdwicks survive are generally more severe than those in which the Swaledale thrives.

One of the best known Herdwick breeders was Beatrix Potter. She simply adored them. In this she was encouraged by Canon Hardwicke Rawnsley. He was a remarkable Cumbrian, who fought hard to keep railways out of the Lake District. He also encouraged the lighting of bonfires on Lakeland mountain tops to celebrate special occasions. It was

Springtime on the Northern Lakeland fells and a shepherd and his faithful dog tend Herdwick sheep and their lambs. Herdwicks are a hardy breed of coarse-wooled sheep that are at home on the fells of Lakeland.

Swaledales, not as hardy as the Herdwicks, here seen ready for clipping.

he who in 1899 founded the Herdwick Sheep Breeders' Association which is still going strong today.

Herdwicks have been part of the Lakeland scene since the twelfth century and, thanks in part to Beatrix Potter, Canon Rawnsley and the Herdwick Sheep Breeders' Association, their future seems assured.

## LAKELAND'S BEST KNOWN LOCAL SPORTS

Two of the oldest of the traditional Lakeland fell-country sports are fox-hunting and Cumberland and Westmorland Wrestling.

Chasing foxes has been part of the daily life of farmers for centuries, done more to protect their sheep and lambs than for the sporting pleasure it brings. Unlike Shire hunting, Lakeland fox-hunting was, for the most part, carried out on foot. Throughout

Cumberland farmers, on horseback, with foxhounds, passing cottages at Ratten Row, in about 1950. When hunting on the Lakeland heights, they would have been on foot. Huntsman Ted Norton is leading the pack.

Cumberland and Westmorland Wrestling champions, Ted Dunglinson and Tommy Little.

any winter fox-hunting season, the numbers of foxes killed was just sufficient to keep their population at a constant level; and all foxes either escaped unharmed or were killed.

Cumberland and Westmorland Wrestling probably dates back to Viking times. It comprises of two men, dressed in embroidered trunks, white tights and vests, grappling and attempting to unbalance each other. If both men fall, the winner is the one on top.

Cumberland and Westmorland Wrestling has its own vocabulary of holds and grips, like the 'hype', the 'hank' and the 'cross buttock'. The winner is declared 'World Champion'.

## MORE LOCAL SPORTS

The whole of the Lake District is a special place, an area of spectacular and craggy fells, beautiful lakes, tarns and neat farms. It is a place where the land is used diversely, and the people who live there work in a multiplicity of ways.

When work is done there are many means of relaxing that are peculiar to Lakeland and somewhat different from other areas.

Cumberland and Westmorland Wrestling is the best-known of the local sports with hound trailing equally popular. Devised from hunting foxes, a trail is set across several miles of countryside. The trail is made by dragging an aniseed-soaked rag which the released dogs follow. Their owners stand at the finishing line, encouraging them and bets

Wrestlers at Grasmere sports, 1907.

Hounds gathering at Calbeck village green on the centenary of John Peel's death.

The Spit Stain (Stone), Caldbeck.

are placed on the participating dogs. These events take place almost every week during spring and summer. The fox-hunting season proper always took place during the winter months until it became illegal to hunt foxes with hounds.

Fell running is cross-country running on the fells and is a really tough sport. Shepherds are usually very good fell runners. The distances of fell runners at local shows are usually shorter than standard fell runs, although these shorter routes are often across very uneven ground so are just as difficult as the longer ones.

An unusual Cumbrian pastime is spitting at a spit stone. The set up is similar to darts but instead of throwing darts at a dartboard, the competitor spits at a spit stone set in a wall.

Cattle at the Cumberland Show, Bitts Park, Carlisle, in about 1960.

The two most important sporting events to take place in Cumbria are the shows at Ambleside and Grasmere.

## FESTIVALS AND SHOWS

Lakeland is made up of Cumberland and Westmorland, two ancient counties which contain festivals and shows that are centuries old. They also have modern revivals of past events. All of them are a celebration of rural tradition which, down the years, has been proudly respected. Most of these very popular events take place in the open air

For anyone who does not enjoy heights, but would like to be close to Heaven, Grasmere Church pictured here, makes a fine refuge. The rush-bearing ceremony is still held there annually.

The wishing gate at Grasmere. Make a wish while leaning on the gate and your wish will come true.

during the summer months and are regular calendar dates which are always claimed in the *Cumberland and Westmorland Herald*.

The oldest festival is the annual rush-bearing ceremony which commemorates the renewal of the rushes which were laid on the earth floor of the church every August and taken up in the spring. Today, crosses made out of rushes are carried by boys and bunches of flowers are carried by the girls who walk in procession, led by a band and followed by the local clergy. The procession ends at the churches where prayers are said and hymns are sung. Rush-bearing dates vary. Musgrave rush-bearing is held on the last Saturday in July while nearby Warcop rush-bearing is on St Peter's day, 29 June. If that date falls on a Sunday, the rush-bearing is held on Saturday 28 June. There are local variations to a rush-bearing ceremony. At Warcop, for example, the event is accompanied by children's sports and a military band.

Egremont Crab Fair, held annually since 1267, features the World Gurning Championship (where contestants wear a horse-collar and pull faces), greasy pole climbing, a pipe-smoking competition and the Biggest Liar in the World competition.

On the third Saturday in August, Carlisle Great Fair begins at the open-air market in the city centre and lasts for ten days. The daily events are announced at the Tourist Information Centre.

Agricultural shows, like the one in Bitts Park, Carlisle, feature farming equipment, craft and trade displays including drystone walling, sheep-shearing competitions, vegetable growing and food stalls. These festivals and shows bind local communities together in a most enjoyable way.

## CUMBRIA'S SIX FOX-HUNTING PACKS

The prime concern of the Cumbrian fox-hunting farmers was control of the foxes that killed their sheep. From their point of view, foxes are vicious killers that, given the chance, kill for the sake of killing. If a fox manages to enter a hen hut, he will kill all the hens in it and simply leave the dead hens where they have fallen.

The hounds used by the Cumbrian farmers are a different breed from those used against southern foxes; and when fox-hunting on the fells, no horses were used. The terrain is unsuitable for horses.

The only member of the Cumbrian pack who wore a red coat is the huntsman.

There were six fox-hunting packs working in Cumbria. The premier pack was the one at Blencathra. It was established in 1840 and its territory includes the countryside around Thirlmere, Derwent Water, Skiddaw and Caldbeck. The north-west fells and beyond them to the coast were covered by the Melbreak pack. The Ullswater pack covered Kentmere, Fairfield and the land towards Penrith. Eskdale and Ennerdale pack operated in south-west Lakeland, Scafell and on to Langdale and the coast. Coniston pack dealt with the Central Lakes and east of Windermere, while the Lunesdale pack operated in the north Pennines.

Before the ban, the fox-hunting season started at the beginning of October and continued until the end of April. Foxes were not hunted during the breeding season.

Fine North Lakeland farmland that was also good fox-hunting country.

Northern Lakeland farmers with their foxhounds. Mr C.N. Parry is on the grey horse.

Tommy Dobson, huntsman of Eskdale Foxhounds, with his pet fox in 1905. Tommy 'crost' (went over) three times in one day, as did the fox.

Skelton, near Penrith. The Ullswater pack hunts in the Skelton area.

## LAKELAND COUNTRYSIDE

Lakeland is a special place, an area of intrinsic beauty that incorporates spectacular and craggy fells, tarns, lakes and lovely little vales. For many centuries it has been a source of inspiration for writers, painters and naturalists and it continues to give enjoyment to millions of visitors who take much pleasure from this splendid and beautiful countryside.

The Lake District is also a place where people live and work and have developed their own customs and folklore. It is a place with its own distinct heritage.

Farming has been present in Lakeland in one shape or another since prehistoric times. Much of Lakeland's appearance today is the result of traditional farming practices. The shape of the fields, drystone walls, hedgerows, vernacular farm buildings, woodlands and copses that so enrich the landscape are all testimony to the importance of farming. Lakeland farms are not at all like the large arable farms common in other parts of the country. They are small and many of them have belonged to the same farming family for centuries. Ninety-three Lakeland farms have been purchased by the National Trust, which is dedicated to preserving traditional Lakeland farms.

Sheep on Cumbrian farm land.

Threshing day on a Lakeland farm, 1910.

A Cumberland farmer and his wife, 1900.

The trust also owns about 30,000 Herdwick sheep, many of which were left to the trust by Beatrix Potter. She also gifted a number of farms to the National Trust. More than any other sheep, the Herdwick is at home on the Lakeland Fells. It is part of the scenery.

Another important feature of Lakeland is its woodland, which includes plantations. There are some 67 acres of woodland in Lakeland. It is an important Lakeland feature.

Taken together, Northern Lakeland's local aspects blend into an area of outstanding natural beauty.

# Further Reading

Blake, Brian, *The Solway Firth*, Robert Hale, 1959

Davies, Hunter, *Beatrix Potter's Lakeland*, Frederick Warne, 1988

——. *The Good Guide To The Lakes*, Foster Davies Ltd, 1984

Davis, R.V., *Geology of Cumbria*, Dalesman Books, 1977

Donaghy, Peter and Laidler, John, *Lakeland Church Walks*, Sigma Leisure, 2001

Hardy, Eric, *The Naturalist In Lakeland*, David and Charles, 1973

Harris, Robert, *Walks In Ancient Lakeland*, Sigma Leisure 2001

*Long, Peter, The Hidden Places of the Lake District And Cumbria*, Travel Publishers, 1990

McCord, Norman and Thompson, Richard, *Northern Counties From 1,000*, Longman, 1998

Wainwright, A., *The Northern Fells*, Westmorland Gazette, 1961